25 Stupid MISTAKES DOG OWNERS MAKE

25 Stupid MISTAKES DOG OWNERS MAKE

by Janine Adams

LOWELL HOUSE

LOS ANGELES

NTC/Contemporary Publishing Group

Library of Congress Cataloging-in-Publication Data
Adams, Janine.
25 stupid mistakes dog owners make / by Janine Adams.
p. cm.
ISBN 0-7373-0490-1 (alk. paper)
1. Dogs—Training. 2. Dogs—Behavior. 3. Dogs.
I. Title: Twenty-five stupid mistakes dog owners make. II. Title.
SF431 .A32 2000
636.7'0887—dc21
00-055374

Published by Lowell House
A division of NTC/Contemporary Publishing Group, Inc.
4255 West Touhy Avenue, Lincolnwood (Chicago), Illinois 60712-1975 U.S.A.

Lowell House books can be purchased at special discounts when ordered in bulk for premiums and special sales. Contact Department CS at the following address:
4255 West Touhy Avenue
Lincolnwood, Illinois 60712-1975
1-800-323-4900

Roxbury Park is an imprint of NTC/Contemporary Publishing Group, Inc.

Managing Director and Publisher: Jack Artenstein
Editor in Chief: Roxbury Park Books: Michael Artenstein
Director of Publishing Services: Rena Copperman
Senior Editor: Maria Magallanes
Editorial Assistant: Nicole Monastirsky
Interior Design: Anna Christian

Printed in the United States of America
International Standard Book Number: 0-7373-0490-1
00 01 02 03 04 DHD 10 9 8 7 6 5 4 3 2 1

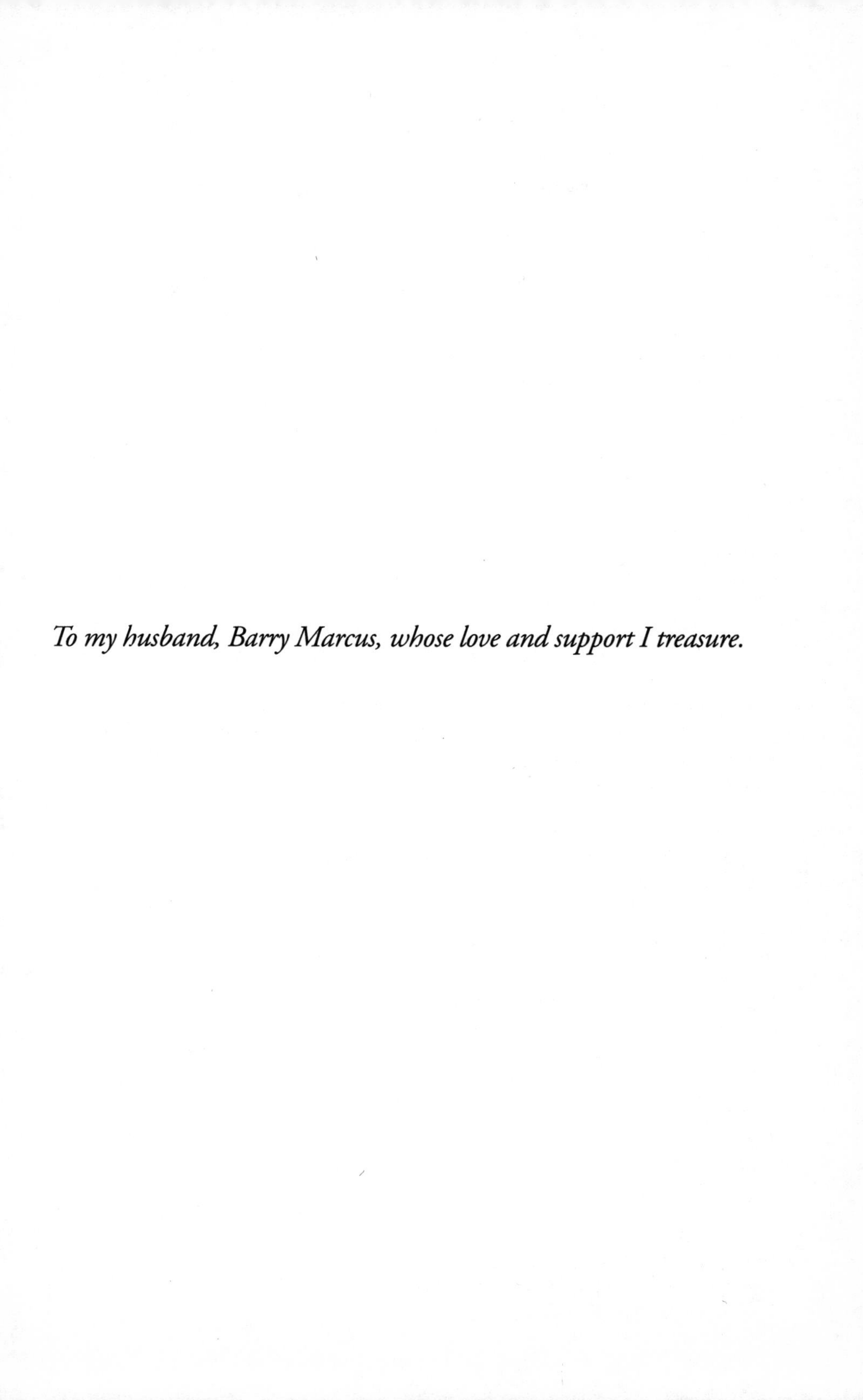

To my husband, Barry Marcus, whose love and support I treasure.

Contents

Acknowledgments

I couldn't have written this book so easily if I hadn't made so many mistakes along the road to responsible dog ownership. I'd like to thank my husband, Barry Marcus, for making those mistakes with me, for growing with me, and for being as devoted to our dogs as I am. I'd also like to thank our poodles, Kramer and Scout, who never once held all those mistakes against us and continue to love us unconditionally.

The experts I consulted for this book were gracious and generous with their time and information. Thank you. The knowledgeable dog owners willing to share their insights and experiences helped enrich the book and ground it in reality. Thanks go to them, too. And I'd like to express special thanks to my on-line canine family, the good folks and dogs of canine-1. Each one of you contributed to this book, whether or not you're mentioned by name. You all have enriched my life immensely. I wish I could meet each of you in person.

Thanks as well to Rachel Livsey, formerly of Lowell House, who assigned this book to me and helped me through the early stages, as well as Lowell House editors Maria Magallanes and Nicole Monastirsky. I'd also like to thank my agent, Mike Snell, for all his good advice and support.

Introduction

When my husband and I bought our first dog, a nine-week-old black standard poodle puppy we named Kramer, I knew next to nothing about dogs. Sure, I'd been to the library to check out the appropriate "dog" books. But I had no practical experience with dogs, and I soon discovered that my instincts weren't right on target. They've been sharply honed in the years since.

Back in 1992, I had some ill-conceived, preconceived notions of what made sense in dog raising. (Don't ask me where those notions came from.) For example, I didn't like the idea of putting my puppy in a cage, and training with treats seemed like it would result in a dog who loved treats, not me.

So I found the training books that matched those ideals (I won't name them here), and, as I followed the advice in those books, I endured a week of puppy hell. I didn't know which way was up, and neither did Kramer.

One week into the ordeal, I walked into the kitchen with my 12-pound puppy attached to my pant leg to answer the phone. It was my husband, Barry, calling to check on how we were doing. "You have to do something!" I cried in desperation. "Bring home a squirt gun or something that will give me some control over this little monster!"

Barry stopped at the local pet-supply store and earnestly told the clerk, "We don't know what to do about our dog. He bites us, he pees in the house, and he doesn't do anything we ask." The clerk looked concerned. "That sounds serious. How old is your dog?" When Barry told her he was ten weeks old, the clerk burst into laughter and handed him the business card of a local obedience school. "You need puppy kindergarten!" she said. "At ten weeks old, he's *supposed* to be doing all those things."

What a difference a few years makes. Looking back, I'm astounded at how little I knew (though I did know enough to acquire a highly trainable breed), and amazed by how much I've learned since. I'm going to try to help you to keep from making the many mistakes I made.

Kramer turned out to be a well-behaved, if slightly neurotic, adult dog. When he was three, I quit my job at a botanical garden to pursue a dream Kramer created for me: becoming a freelance dog writer.

Over the past five years of writing newspaper, magazine, and Web site articles, as well as books, I've had the chance to ask some of the nation's dog experts for the answers to my questions. I'm signed up on some great Internet mailing lists, so I've become acquainted with hundreds of experienced, knowledgeable, responsible dog owners. You know what? Most of them have made at least some of the mistakes this book describes.

Rest assured, the information in this book comes from hard experience—my own and that of others. By reading it and implementing the ideas included here, you can benefit from that experience without having to live through the same mistakes.

Incidentally, another black standard poodle, Scout, joined our family four years ago. She was three when she came to live with us, and she didn't turn our lives upside down the way young Kramer did. Though the two dogs are the same breed, they have entirely different personalities, and Scout has brought along her own set of challenges. But each is wonderful in his and her own way, and both have taught me so much about dogs (and other things). I truly couldn't have written this book without them.

My hope is that *25 Stupid Mistakes Dog Owners Make* will help to prevent you from making some big mistakes with your own dog (or potential dog). It sets up an ideal for treating your dog as a thinking, feeling, full-fledged member of your family. That's not a difficult ideal to live up to. And if you do, you're bound to gain a lot.

1 Do Your Homework

If you think you're ready to acquire a canine soul mate, one of the best things you can do for your new pet—and for yourself—is to take the time to ask yourself some serious questions, do some research, and acquire the right dog.

As a living creature who will share your life for a dozen years or more, a dog should never be purchased on an impulse. No matter how cute that puppy in the window is, or how badly you feel for your colleague's neighbor—who must find a new home for his dog—don't take on responsibility for a new dog without first examining your life to make sure you're ready, then doing research to figure out the right dog for you.

▸ DON'T ACQUIRE THE WRONG DOG ◂

Before you open your heart and home to a specific dog, examine these questions:

Are You Ready?

A dog is a lifetime commitment. If you bring a dog into your life, please do so with the determination that yours will be the last home this dog will have. Your dog will love you unconditionally. You should love him in return. He does not deserve to be treated as a disposable commodity.

Bearing in mind that you may be responsible for this animal for a dozen or more years, look at your lifestyle to determine whether it can accommodate a dog.

- Do you have enough money to take good care of a dog, even if he should become ill or injured?
- Are you away from your home for twelve hours or more a day?
- Do you travel frequently?
- Will you be undergoing any foreseeable transitions in your life, which might be difficult if you have a dog?
- Do you have enough space in your home for a dog?

If you can respond honestly to questions like these and still feel that your life can accommodate a dog, and that you're ready for the commitment, the next step is to start thinking about the type of dog that would best suit you.

Are you attracted to large or small dogs? Each has its attributes. Many people (like me) enjoy the presence of a sizable dog. But small dogs have many advantages, too: You can scoop them up if trouble looms, they can hang out on your lap without crushing you, and you can travel with them more easily.

Coat considerations are also important. A golden retriever is luxurious to the touch, but staying on top of the dog hair he sheds becomes a big part of your life. Short-coated dogs also shed a lot. Poodles and other minimally shedding breeds generally require time-consuming or expensive grooming.

Finally, think about how you want to spend time with your dog. If you're hoping to take him jogging, you'll want an athletic breed. On the other hand, if you're a couch potato, a dog who needs less exercise might be appropriate, although all dogs need a certain amount of exercise (see chapter 9). All these factors should be considered carefully to ensure that you and your dog are the right "fit."

Purebred or Mixed Breed?

It's an age-old question. Do you spend a lot of money for a purebred dog, or do you roll the dice and adopt a mixed breed? Both purebreds and mutts have their proponents.

Because mixed-breed dogs are not bred with close relatives, they are often more stable in terms of health and temperament. They make fabulous pets.

When it came time to buy our first dog, my husband and I chose a purebred so that we could have a good idea of what to expect. We selected a breed, the standard poodle, whose temperament seemed to fit ours and whose appearance and size appealed to us. We also wanted a dog that doesn't shed. As novice dog owners, that predictability was important to us.

Buying a Purebred Dog

If predictability appeals to you, do your homework about breeds. Read books that describe individual breeds. Be honest about your lifestyle. Are you active? Sedentary? Will you be able to give your dog a lot of exercise? All these factors (and many more) will help you to select an appropriate dog.

Once you've narrowed things down, go to dog shows to see the breeds that interest you, suggests Chris Walkowicz, a breeder of bearded collies and the author of *The Perfect Match: A Dog Buyer's Guide* and coauthor of *Successful Dog Breeding: The Complete Handbook of Canine Midwifery.* When you see a dog in person, you can touch and feel him, Walkowicz says. You can see how big the breed actually gets. If you're at a dog show, you can also get an idea of the breed's grooming needs, and you can speak with breeders, handlers, and others who are knowledgeable about the breed.

If you opt for a purebred puppy, you simply must do your research and find a responsible breeder who has screened her dogs for genetic problems and temperament, and who is breeding to further the quality of the breed. (I use the female pronoun because breeders are predominantly female.)

That rules out pet shops. Responsible breeders don't sell to pet shops or puppy brokers because they want to be able to choose the buyers for their puppies. A puppy purchased in a pet shop is likely to have come from a commercial puppy producer who breeds without regard for the health or temperament of the parents or puppies.

Pet-shop puppies were likely taken away from their mothers too early. They may have been shipped a great distance under frightening (by puppy standards) conditions, and they've generally been kept in cages, with no attempt at housetraining. This makes them difficult for their new owners to housetrain, since they've become accustomed to sitting among their own feces.

Because purebred dogs can come from limited genetic stock, you should buy from a breeder who has tested her dogs for genetic diseases that could be passed along to the puppies. Your average backyard breeder who bred her beloved pet so that her kids could witness the miracle of birth hasn't gone to that trouble. If you buy from someone who doesn't test her dogs—no matter how nice the breeder is or how cute the puppies are—you might end up caring for a dog with a heart-breaking genetic disease down the road.

Anaclare Evans of Detroit learned this lesson the hard way. Her Bedlington terrier, Farnsie, has an illness called copper toxicosis, a potentially fatal, hereditary disease. Evans advises others to investigate the genetic status of the parents of any puppy they're considering buying. "I did not do this with Farnsie, and as a result, I have a dog with an incurable but controllable genetic disorder," she says.

Here's something important to keep in mind. "Papers," that is, registration with American Kennel Club (AKC), are not a guarantee of quality. The AKC is the first to admit it: The AKC is a registry—and nothing more. Papers from the AKC signify only that the registered puppy was born to registered parents. The AKC relies on breeders to be honest when filling out forms. Registration does not mean the breeder is responsible or that the parents were tested for genetic faults. Papers allow you to compete with your purebred dog in AKC-sponsored sports and activities, as well as to produce AKC-registered puppies. That's it.

Screening the Breeder

We're not trying to discourage you from buying a purebred dog. But after you settle on a breed (after careful research and self-examination), keep doing your homework to find a responsible breeder.

How do you find a responsible breeder? Start by contacting the American Kennel Club, which has a breeder referral service. (Call 900-407-7877, or check out the AKC's Web site at www.akc.org.) But it's up to you to screen any breeders you identify.

How will you know the breeder is responsible? "I think more than anything, you should see a relationship between the person and the dogs," says Walkowicz. Does the breeder treat the puppies like creatures or objects? Walkowicz advises you to keep an eye out for the adoring look the dog gives to the breeder when the breeder isn't even paying attention to her. Watch for the breeder to absentmindedly stroke the dogs while talking with you. "Look for unconscious behavior," Walkowicz says. "Because the conscious behavior can be faked."

The breeder should not only love her own dogs, but she should also love her breed as well. And that love should be readily apparent. Walkowicz advises looking for subtle things, like the breeder wearing a sweatshirt or earrings that depict the breed. These little details can indicate that the breeder really loves the breed.

Other hallmarks of a reputable breeder include titles on their dogs (initials before and after the registered name—ask the breeder what the initials stand for), health guarantees, and a willingness (or insistence) to take back the dog should you have to find a new home for him.

A good breeder will also scrutinize you. Don't be surprised if the breeder interviews you more than you interview her. A good breeder is much more interested in ensuring that her beloved puppies are placed in excellent homes than in making the sale.

If you visit the breeder, and the breeder doesn't fit these criteria, or you have any hesitation, don't buy the dog. It's difficult to walk away from an adorable puppy, but you want to buy one with a good temperament, one that comes from healthy genetic stock. You want to buy from a breeder who will be there for you if you have questions or concerns as your dog grows up. So don't be afraid to leave empty-handed. If red flags go up, "turn tail and walk out of there," Walkowicz advises.

What About a Mixed Breed?

Much of the general public believes that if a dog doesn't have a pedigree, there's something wrong with him, says Walkowicz. Even the word *mutt*, which is short for "muttonhead," is derogatory. Mixed-breed dogs are the second-class citizens of the dog world, says Karen Derrico, author of *Unforgettable Mutts: Pure of Heart, Not of Breed.*

Derrico is out to polish the image of the mixed-breed dog (she cites a more appropriate acronym for the term: *Most Unique Totally Terrific dog*). "If you polled a group of veterinarians and asked them which dogs are healthier (pure or mixed breeds), I'm pretty sure the majority would say mutts," she says. That's certainly borne out in Sydney Armstrong's family. Armstrong of Raleigh, North Carolina, has two beagles and two mixed-breed dogs. Her beagles have health concerns like dental problems, allergies, and epilepsy, while her mixes are free of ongoing health problems.

One of the joys of having a mutt is that she's a unique specimen. "Each has a genuine look all their own, and when you get a puppy, you have no idea what that sweet face will look like when full grown," says Penny Bolton of Colchester, Vermont, the enthusiastic owner of Daisy Mae, a Brittany/English springer spaniel mix.

But unique looks can be a two-edged sword, says Derrico. If you fall in love with a particular dog, chances are you won't be able to get another one that looks just like him (as the owner of a purebred dog can). "That's why I take lots and lots of pictures of my mutts," Derrico says.

(A wealthy couple in Texas is trying to get around this limitation. They're so crazy about their Border collie/husky mix, Missy, that they put up $2.3 million to fund cloning research so that they could get another one just like her.)

Another joy of owning a mixed breed is giving a home to a dog that might not readily get one. "My number one reason for having a mixed-breed dog over a purebred is that they exist in much too great a quantity. Someone has to love them," says Eileen Reidinger of Columbus, Ohio. "A dog is a dog, and there is no reason that my dog must have a designer label. Love comes with or without a pedigree."

Mutts aren't necessarily better than purebreds, says Derrico. But, except for being less predictable, they're just as good as purebred dogs, and they deserve loving homes. "Every dog should have an equal chance for a home because they all deserve a chance," she says. Dogs love us regardless of our hair color or the tilt of our ears, she adds. We should do the same for them.

Shelter Dogs

If you adopt a dog from a shelter, you get the personal satisfaction of saving a life. We have a serious pet overpopulation problem in this country. Hundreds of thousands of dogs are euthanized each month because they lack homes. Many wonderful, adoptable dogs, both mixed breed and purebred, are waiting at the shelter for the perfect home. The background and ancestry of your shelter dog may be a mystery to you, but your future together can be wonderful.

The challenge is in selecting your shelter dog. The shelter environment can be so stressful that it's difficult for a dog to show her true colors. "You do need to be careful with a shelter dog," says dog trainer Pat Miller, author of *The Common Sense Approach: Positive Dog Training*, who worked in animal shelters for years.

Miller thinks that slightly sensitive dogs make great pets. The problem is that these dogs might not show well in a shelter. They won't be the dogs dashing to the front of the kennel run, saying "take me home." The slightly sensitive dogs are sitting in their kennels, looking intimidated. "These dogs don't look good in shelters," she says. "They may be reasonably well-socialized, just sensitive."

A good shelter will have a place where you can take the dog so that you can have some time together in a calmer environment. Ideally, you'll be able to take the dog off-leash to see how he reacts. He may be so bold and confident that he'll want nothing to do with you, says Miller. A more sensitive dog will seek your attention.

If you have kids, or if your new dog will be around children, Miller advises you to take a child with you to the shelter, so that you can gauge how the dog will do with kids. Due to prior bad experiences, some shelter dogs are afraid of children.

Selecting a progressive shelter can make the adoption process easier. "Although you can find a good dog in any shelter, I would steer people toward the more progressive shelters that are doing puppy testing and trying to match people with the proper dog," says Gina Spadafori, syndicated pet-care columnist and author of *Dogs for Dummies.* "Instead of just telling you to go back to the cages and pick out what you want, these shelters do preinterviews; they know the animals they have there, and they're doing their best to make sure that what goes out doesn't come back," she says. Progressive shelters offer counseling afterward and give you follow-up support.

A shelter dog should be no more an impulse "buy" than a puppy you get from a breeder. It can be difficult for some people to walk out of a shelter empty-handed. If you are one of those people, be sure you've carefully considered adopting a dog before you head for your local shelter. Know that you are ready, and don't take home a particular dog if you're not sure he's the right one. Listen to both your heart and your head.

Purebred Rescue Groups

Another source for acquiring a purebred dog, usually an adult, is a purebred rescue group. These comprise breeders and lovers of a particular breed who help homeless dogs of that breed. Many responsible breeders participate in rescue as a way to give back to the breed.

Rescue dogs have usually spent some time in a foster home for evaluation, so if you acquire one, you can get some information in advance on what she's like. You'll know, for instance, whether she's good with cats or kids, something that's difficult to learn about a shelter dog until you get her home.

Rescue dogs don't usually come with pedigrees, so you run the risk of acquiring a purebred with genetic problems. But you're helping a homeless pet in need. Most rescue and shelter dogs have been neutered (or you'll be required to neuter them), so don't consider rescue a source for a breeding animal. (Before you decide that you want to breed, read chapter 20.)

Rescue groups will probably screen you as carefully as would a breeder selling you a puppy. Camille Partridge, a breeder of Scottish terriers under the kennel name Gaelforce, for example, uses the same criteria (and the same contract) for adopters of rescue dogs as she does for puppy buyers. If you're interested in an AKC breed, consult the AKC for the name of the breed club's rescue coordinator.

Puppy or Adult?

Should you acquire a puppy or an adult dog? There are advantages to both.

If you get a puppy, you can control her experiences during her formative weeks and months. You can make sure she's well socialized. (See chapter 7 on the importance of socialization.) You also get to accept the blame for any neuroses she develops.

Puppies are cute as the dickens. They're also a whole lot of work. They can turn your life upside down. "Getting a puppy is exactly like having a baby," says author Walkowicz. When we acquired Kramer at the age of nine weeks, I took two weeks off from my job. At the end of the first week, my friend-colleague came over to meet the puppy. She says she's never seen the mother of a newborn baby look more exhausted than I did that day. (For advice on raising a puppy, see chapter 2.)

With an adult dog, what you see is what you get, says Walkowicz. You know how big your dog will be, how much he sheds, whether he's shy or outgoing. The dog may well be housetrained already (or, if not, he'll be easier to housetrain than a puppy). But when you acquire an adult dog, there's still that question mark about his background—an older animal will come with his own "baggage."

Scout was three when she joined our family, after having been saved by a vet who didn't comply with her owners' wishes to euthanize her after she was hit by a car. She integrated herself seamlessly into our family.

When you get a dog, ideally you will keep him for his entire life. But sometimes life gets in the way. What if circumstances beyond your control dictate that you find your dog a new home? That can happen; and if it does, you owe it to your dog to find the best situation for him you possibly can. Chapter 24 offers advice on what to do if you simply must find a new home for your dog.

The biggest mistake people make when it comes to getting a dog is that they either get one when they're not ready for a pet, they get the wrong dog for their lifestyle, or they get a dog from a bad source. "You can make the most intelligent breed selection in the world, but if you don't get it from a reputable source, you might just as well have not bothered," says pet expert Spadafori. "An AKC golden retriever isn't like a Sony video camera. You can't pick the brand and then go shop for the price."

If you're considering getting a dog, take your time, and do the research. It's time well spent on a decision that you'll live with for a dozen years or more.

2 Start Off on the Right Foot

Puppies are undeniably adorable, which is lucky for them, because sometimes their looks are the only thing that keep us from wanting to kill them! A new puppy can wreak havoc on your life. The constant supervision, the housetraining, the little battles over chewed shoes, destroyed furniture, and anything else he can get his little mouth on—it's all exhausting. It needn't be that way, says veterinarian and animal behaviorist Ian Dunbar, Ph.D., MRCVS, author of *How to Teach a New Dog Old Tricks* and the director of the SIRIUS Puppy Training program. He says that by using three simple techniques (socialization, confinement, and bite-inhibition training), you can keep your puppy out of trouble and retain your sanity. Most importantly, you can help to mold a puppy into a dog who is a joy to live with.

▸ DON'T SQUANDER THE FIRST WEEKS WITH YOUR PUPPY ◂

The ideal time to bring a puppy home from her mother is at eight weeks. This gives the puppy adequate time with her mother and littermates to learn how to play and to learn that bites hurt! Puppies who are taken from their mothers too early can become problem dogs.

The period between the age of eight weeks and three months is your golden opportunity to expose your puppy to a wide variety of people and experiences so that she won't grow up to be a fearful dog. This is called socialization, and it's so important that an entire chapter in this book is devoted to it. But it bears emphasizing that if you have a puppy, socializing her well should be a priority.

"If you will do only one thing for your puppy, early socialization is probably the most important step you can take to save your dog's life," says Pat Miller. "Anything you do later can't compare to the value of early socialization. You miss out on those important early weeks if you wait."

Dunbar recommends that between eight and twelve weeks, your puppy meet one hundred people. The interaction with those people must be positive and include training, he says. (See chapter 7 for a detailed description of Dunbar's puppy-socialization program.)

Dunbar also recommends puppy kindergarten for socializing your puppy to other dogs but notes that kindergarten should be a continuation, not the beginning, of the socialization process. (Many puppy classes don't accept puppies younger than three months.) "You don't take your puppy to puppy class to socialize him; you take him to puppy class to continue socializing an already socialized puppy," Dunbar says.

Housetraining

Teaching your puppy to go to the bathroom outside is a priority for all dog owners. It requires your diligence, but it's time well spent. Failure to housetrain can have disastrous results. Many animals have landed in shelters because their owners deemed them impossible to housetrain.

In his book, *How to Teach a New Dog Old Tricks,* Dunbar outlines a housetraining method that actually helps the puppy to train himself. The beauty of this method is that it doesn't allow for the puppy to make mistakes in the house. If you follow each step, you'll have a housetrained puppy within a few weeks' time, even if (or especially if) you leave the puppy alone while you go to work.

When You're Not Home: Long-Term Confinement

When you're not home, Dunbar recommends that you place your puppy in a long-term confinement area, like a bathroom or other room that provides little for the puppy to damage. Remove all chewable items, like the shower curtain, rug, and toilet paper. Place these items in the room: a dog bed, a water dish with fresh water, some chew toys stuffed with the puppy's breakfast, and a doggie toilet.

The doggie toilet should be placed as far away from the bed as possible, at the diagonally opposite corner of the room. It should be made of the same material (or substrate, as Dunbar calls it) that you want your animal to eliminate on outside. If you want your dog to go to the bathroom on grass, buy a roll of sod and put down a piece in your long-term confinement area. If you expect your dog to go on the sidewalk or patio, bring in thin concrete slabs. "Puppies quickly develop a strong preference for eliminating on the type of substrate they eliminated on when they were young," Dunbar explains.

Why a long-term confinement area and not a crate or cage? Dunbar's method does use a crate (more on that a little later), but a young puppy's bladder has about a seventy-five-minute capacity, he says. If you plan to be away for longer than an hour, put the puppy where he can go to the bathroom. If you force him to soil in his crate, you ruin the crate's usefulness as a housetraining tool.

So when you're away from home, put the puppy in his long-term confinement zone. "This eradicates any mistakes around the house," says Dunbar. "You have an error-free management system." The puppy will naturally want to use his dog toilet, because he'll want to go to the bathroom as far as possible from his bed. "By locking your puppy up all day while you're at work, he's basically teaching himself to want to do it on grass."

When you come home from work, pick up the feces, and change the sod once a week. Dogs don't like to go where feces are, but the urine smell will attract them to urinate there.

Using the Crate: Short-Term Confinement

The crate, either a wire cage or a plastic airline crate, is a helpful tool for housetraining. Many dogs enjoy their crates and continue to use them well after they've been housetrained (see chapter 11). But here we'll take a look at how Dunbar uses a crate in his housetraining system.

When you are at home, the crate comes in handy as a nifty housetraining tool. Keep your puppy in the crate (with a yummy chew toy), and let him out every hour on the hour (remember, he has to pee every hour). He'll either chew or nap in there, but as soon as you let him out, there's every chance in the world that he'll have to pee.

So open the door, clip on a leash, hustle him outside to the area in which you want him to go to the bathroom, and wait. Within three minutes, he'll doubtless pee, says Dunbar, and in probably one out of two trips, he'll poop. When he does eliminate, praise him, and give him three liver treats. Your dog will quickly learn that eliminating outside gets him treats. The indoor toilet provides only relief, so your dog will use it only out of necessity, when you're not home.

The beauty of using the crate is that you can predict when your dog will have to go to the bathroom. "The crate makes housetraining as easy as falling off a log," says Dunbar, "because all you have to do, every time the big hand hits 12, is to let your puppy out, and run him to his outdoor toilet area." He won't pee in the crate if he can help it—that would be counter to his denning instinct. So if you don't force him to pee in the crate by leaving him there too long, you're guaranteed to have something to praise him about when you take him outside.

Once you've waited your three minutes, and you know he's empty, then you can bring him back inside to play, without worrying that he'll have an accident. After you're through playing, pop the pup back in the crate for about a half hour, until the beginning of the next hour, when you should let him out again.

As your puppy grows and his bladder gets bigger, he will be able to hold his urine longer. When you get home from work, check his indoor toilet. If there are no feces and a blot with a tissue reveals no urine, you're on the right track. Your puppy figures he's better off waiting for you to come home and take him outside to go to the bathroom—that way he'll get treats! After a month without your puppy using his indoor toilet, you can take it away.

You'll also expand your puppy's long-term confinement area, room by room. After an initial two months in one room, add another (or perhaps a hall). Add a room each month, until by the time he's ten or twelve months old, your dog has earned complete freedom in your home.

An important note: Dunbar points out that it's essential for you to continue to go outside with your dog to his toilet area and reward him for using it. This strengthens his desire to go to the bathroom outside rather than inside. It also allows you to check his feces to make sure he's healthy—and to clean them up. Fresh feces pose little health risk to humans, says Dunbar, but worms have had a chance to hatch in days-old feces, making them much more dangerous to humans. So for hygienic reasons, clean up immediately. This way you'll also avoid the nasty task of the weekly scooping.

The Ex-Pen

Ex-pens (short for exercise pens) are 2-foot-wide, 4-foot-tall sections of wire panels that you can connect together to form a circle to create pens.

Ex-pens can be used to make a larger long-term confinement area, or they can serve as a smaller pen to use as a short-term confinement area, like a bottomless and topless crate. An ex-pen is a great tool for keeping your puppy with the family but out of trouble, says Deborah Wood, a dog trainer and author of *The Tao of Bow Wow.* I interviewed Wood just days after a papillon puppy, Pogo, joined her family. "I cannot imagine having this puppy and not having a crate and an ex-pen," Wood told me. "I don't know how I would housetrain him or keep him from committing suicide."

Wood, who also wrote *Help for Your Shy Dog,* says it's important not to isolate a puppy, particularly a shy one. She uses a crate in the bedroom and an ex-pen in the living room. "I like the idea of an ex-pen, because it is bright and light and part of the world." The puppy can join the family but be safe.

On-Leash Supervision

Dog trainer Andrea Arden, author of *Dog-Friendly Dog Training,* adds on-leash supervision to long-term confinement and short-term confinement (the crate) as the tools needed to mold a well-behaved puppy.

When your puppy is out of his confinement areas and under your supervision, keep her on-leash, she suggests. On-leash supervision can be used in two ways. You can keep the dog at your side, and step on the leash if you need to control him. Or, you can tether the leash to something stable. Some trainers advocate tying the leash to your waist, like an umbilical cord, but Arden says, she's seen dogs develop separation anxiety with that method. "The dog thinks he has to follow the owner around all the time."

When your puppy is tethered to a table—while you sit in the room with him—give him something to chew on to occupy his time. This teaches him that he doesn't always have to be active in the house.

By using each of these three methods of confinement, your puppy can't get into trouble. "Part of the reason puppies are so exhausting is that if you don't manage them properly, they're always getting into trouble," Arden says. "So a good 70 percent of the time you're with your puppy, you're upset." If you use long-term confinement, short-term confinement, and on-leash supervision—along with lots of chew toys—you won't spend your time being angry. (It almost makes me want to get a puppy just to try it!)

Make Your Puppy a Kong-aholic—Nip Chewing in the Bud

The long-term confinement area takes care of another annoying puppy practice: chewing. Dunbar suggests you stock the room with hollow chew toys stuffed with kibble. Hard, hollow, rubber Kong toys work well for this task, as do hollowed-out, sterilized bones. Kong makes toys that stand up to even the toughest chewers, but be sure to inspect them periodically to see that no cracks have developed. If they have, replace the toy so that your dog doesn't break it apart and swallow (or choke on) the pieces when you're not home.

After you stuff the toy, you can put a plug of peanut butter on the end to hold in the kibble. Feed your puppy's breakfast to him this way. "As he chews, little bits of kibble fall out, thus rewarding him for playing on his chew toys," explains Dunbar. He'll spend a couple of hours chewing on his toy and eating his kibble. Then he'll promptly fall asleep.

The result? "Within three to four days, the dog basically becomes a Kong-aholic." He is so focused on his chew toys he doesn't want to chew anything else. "He never gets treats out of the couch or the remote control, like he does out of the Kong," says Dunbar.

If your puppy is enjoying a chew toy, not only is he not chewing the couch, but he's also not barking, running around, or getting all worked up because his

▼ POOCH POINTER ▼

Following is a four-stage bite-inhibition training process from Dunbar's How to Teach an Old Dog New Tricks:

STAGE ONE: *Play with your puppy in his long-term confinement area. Let him mouth you in play sessions. Whenever it hurts, let him know by saying "ouch!" Stop playing for one minute. If he comes back and mouths you again, yelp again, and leave him. After a minute, call him to you, and if he mouths you again, walk away for three minutes. You've taken away his ultimate reward: your attention.*

STAGE TWO: *Don't wait for it to hurt. Whenever he mouths you, even when it's a soft bite, pretend it hurts, and go through the above procedure. Gradually lower your threshold for a yelp, until you're yelping without any pressure whatsoever. "This way, the puppy learns to be gentle with humans," says Dunbar. "You've totally taken the force out of the bite."*

STAGE THREE: *Now you're ready to work on the frequency. You get the puppy to stop when you say so. Teach him this by using the "off" request. Hold a treat in your closed fist, say "off," wait for the puppy to move his nose away from your hand, and then give him the treat. You can use "off" with the mouthing. Say his name, "off," and have him sit. If he sits, he can start mouthing again. When you tire of the game, give him a stuffed Kong to play with.*

STAGE FOUR: *Teach your dog never to bite you, except when you ask him to. Teach him a sequence of events, called a "combination command," which must take place before he can mouth you. (This way, you don't risk someone accidentally asking him to bite.) For example, he must be lying down, hear his name, then hear a ridiculous command (Dunbar uses "kill me"). You can be fairly certain that no one will accidentally say "kill me" to your dog. Dunbar periodically checks his adult dogs to make sure their bite inhibition is still low. He takes them through the combination command. If there's* any *pressure, he says "ouch!"*

parents have left him for the day. He learns to enjoy his own company. It's a great way to prevent your puppy from suffering from separation anxiety when you leave your house.

Once you've returned from work, have exercised your puppy, and prepared to crate him for a while, put his supper in a chew toy, and give it to him in his crate, suggests Dunbar. He should settle down nicely.

Mouthing: Ouch!

If you use the confinement and chew-toy tips just mentioned, you will really only be faced with one more annoying puppy habit: mouthing. Puppies have razor-sharp teeth, so you must teach them how hard they can bite before it hurts you. This is called bite inhibition. Other dogs do a great job of telling one another when they've bitten too hard: They yelp (which is one reason puppy kindergarten is so helpful). But it's your job to teach your puppy that tender human hands should not be bitten.

You do that not by discouraging mouthing but actually by encouraging it, says Dunbar. The important thing to remember is that you must teach the puppy to inhibit the force of his bite before you teach him to limit its frequency. Many people discourage a puppy the first time he mouths. He learns not to bite them, but he never learns how to soften his bite. If you inhibit the force of his bite when he's a puppy, if he does bite you later in life (should you slam the door on his tail, for example), he won't bite too hard. Otherwise, he might really do some damage.

As you raise your puppy, remember that what you teach now will stick with him for a lifetime. If you don't want your dog to mouth you when he's an adult, don't allow him to do it as a puppy (after you've inhibited the bite). The same goes for jumping up on you and other potentially annoying habits.

Puppyhood is fleeting—be sure to take advantage of it.

3 Be Fair

If I were a dog, the one thing I think I'd really miss (besides thumbs) is the ability to control my life. Dogs have so little say over what they get to do. They have to turn to us for everything. In the absence of a dog door, it's the human who decides when the dog goes out or in. The human also decides when and what the dog will eat. And, let's face it, humans expect dogs to bow to our whims.

That's just the nature of the human/dog relationship. We lead them. If we don't, and the dog tries to take control, it upsets the balance. (For more on the importance of leadership, see chapter 12.) We're the leaders—but we must be benevolent leaders and set fair rules for our dogs to live by.

▸ DON'T IGNORE YOUR DOG'S NEED FOR STABILITY AND CONSISTENCY ◂

If you're like most people, you work away from home. Your dog is alone from nine to five (or longer). With any luck, she enjoys chew toys, and you've left some fun ones for her. Hopefully, she's had a nice walk before work, so she's tired and will sleep while you're gone. But chances are good that just before the time you usually get home, she will wake up and eagerly await your return.

Stick to Routine, with Room for Flexibility

Dogs have amazing internal clocks. My dogs eat breakfast around 10:15 A.M., about forty-five minutes after we return from our morning walk in the park. I'm lucky enough to work from home, so I just stop what I'm doing at about that time and feed them. But if I'm occupied, or if I lose track of time, I can count on my chowhound, Scout, to remind me. And it's almost always right around 10:15. Her reminder starts with an intense stare and maybe a whimper, and if I don't heed either, it turns into an insistent bark. She doesn't appreciate my messing with her schedule.

It will be easier on your dog if you can come home from work at roughly the same time every day so he doesn't spend too much time anticipating your arrival. One of the rules you've probably set for your dog is that he has to wait for you to come home and take him out rather than eliminating in the house. It's not fair if your dog has to hold it several extra hours while you go to happy hour with your coworkers. It's a good idea to give an extra key to a trusted neighbor, friend, or professional dog walker, so that in the event you're detained at work, someone will be able to come in and let your dog out.

While they do have finely calibrated internal clocks, dogs are also pretty flexible. "I think dogs are among the most adaptable creatures on earth," says pet-care columnist Gina Spadafori. Most people have two set routines—one on weekdays, the other on weekends. "Dogs go effortlessly and fluently between the two," she says.

When I travel with my dogs, and their schedules are messed up, it doesn't seem to bother them—they go with the flow. Still, I think it's nice to stick (more or less) to a routine if one has been established. Consider your dog before making major changes. They have so little control over what happens to them that routine can make life feel more stable.

If your dog isn't used to a routine, he can be a lot more flexible. Susan Bemus of Flagstaff, Arizona, a responsible owner of eleven dogs (primarily Bernese mountain dogs and Cardigan Welsh corgis), believes that it's best for you to avoid ingraining a routine into your dog's psyche. She and her husband keep their dogs on a loose schedule—feeding within a two-hour range of times, for example. "The dogs begin telling us at 7:00 A.M. and 5:00 P.M. that they think it's time for walks and meals, but they easily accept it if we switch the timing around."

The Bemuses don't have a work regimen, and they don't want the dogs to have a routine simply for the sake of having one. "There really is little that is routine about our lives, and it works best for all of us to teach the dogs to be adaptable rather than to create an artificial routine for their sakes. That would just end up putting additional stress on the humans and make it harder for us to devote as much of ourselves to the dogs as we do," she explains. The dogs are willing to wait to go for their walk—and they know that their walk always precedes their meal.

The dogs themselves participate in a variety of activities, including conformation, carting, drill team, and therapy work, so their own lives aren't regimented. "It is convenient for us to juggle the dogs' schedule, and the dogs don't seem to mind a bit," says Bemus.

The logic in that is apparent, though most people's work schedules don't have a lot of built-in flexibility. The important thing is not to ask too much of your dog or to put her in a position where she's physically uncomfortable waiting for you to arrive. If your schedule is, by necessity, fairly routine, try not to veer from it too much.

When you're with your dog, you're her rock, and she can look to you as a source of stability. But if she's home waiting for you, be considerate.

Much of what your dog can handle is a result of what she's used to. In other words, if your dog is accustomed to spending nine hours a day alone, she'll be able to handle ten hours more easily than the dog that's only home alone four hours on a typical day.

And, of course, remember that dogs are individuals, so one dog might be more flexible than another, just as some humans are more easygoing than others.

Be Consistent About Rules

When you teach your dog the rules of the household, try to be consistent in enforcing them. It's not fair, for example, to allow your dog to sleep with you one night and shove him off the bed the next. This is a surefire way to confuse your dog. By constantly changing the rules, you undermine your role as his leader. He might decide to start setting the rules himself. Being inconsistent with rules can damage your relationship.

Dog trainer Pat Miller points out that being consistent does not mean being punitive. "Be firm, but not forceful," she advises.

Dogs discriminate well. In other words, a three-minute down stay in the living room feels different to your dog from a three-minute down stay in the obedience ring. That's why good obedience competitors practice those down stays in a variety of environments before trying them out in competition.

You can use that discrimination skill to your advantage if you want to make consistent exceptions to the rules. For example, Barry and I don't allow Kramer and Scout to sleep in our bed with us at home. Two people, two standard poodles, and a queen-size bed is just too crowded. But when we travel, we allow the dogs in bed (we cover the hotel's bedspread with a sheet brought from home). Frequently, hotel rooms have king-size beds (or more than one bed), so there's plenty of room.

In spite of this inconsistency, the dogs have never tried to get on the bed when we're at home. They can tell the difference. The same is true for getting on the furniture: They're not allowed on most of the furniture at home—with the exception of a single couch. They don't have a problem with this distinction. Similarly, if we're visiting friends who allow their dogs on the couch, we'll invite Kramer or Scout up. It doesn't mean they think they can sit on all the couches at home.

Treat Dogs as Individuals

Another disservice we do to our dogs is to expect them to live up to the standards set by another dog. Canines are individuals, just as people are. You're probably very different from your siblings despite having a shared biological heritage and upbringing. Even if your new dog is the same breed as your old one, you can't expect the two to behave in the same way.

My two standard poodles couldn't be more different from one another. Kramer is cautious, dignified, and rather high-strung. The slightest noise bothers him. You don't have to tell him no twice (with the exception of a few ingrained behaviors). Scout is a bossy, scrappy gal, always looking out for "number one"—her. You could drop a dictionary next to her head, and she wouldn't jump. The two make a fabulous pair. But it would be supremely unfair for us to expect Scout to live up to the amazing standards Kramer has set. You could leave a piece of chicken on the dining room table, and Kramer would ignore it. Scout would be all over it in a New York minute.

Even littermates can be different from one another. Sally Brown of O'Fallon, Illinois, has a Great Pyrenees/Border collie cross, Otis, the result of an accidental breeding. Her parents own Otis's littermate, Josie. Despite the fact that the two dogs look alike, they're completely different. Otis is much more like his Great Pyrenees mother, sweet but slow moving and not necessarily a great problem solver. The family slogan is "Otis doesn't notice."

Josie is as sharp as her Border collie father. She figured out how to open latched doors so that she could let herself out to explore her family's large, fenced farmland. She's always busy. Everything about Otis and Josie is different, says Brown, except they both can take unlimited amounts of affection.

If you're living with the memory of a beloved dog, don't delude yourself into thinking that you can replace her. Your new dog will doubtless be a marvelous addition to your family. But if you expect her to act just like your prior pet, you're not being fair to the newcomer. You're potentially setting up the new dog for failure and yourself for disappointment. You may well be preventing yourself from appreciating your new dog for her unique virtues.

One of the biggest challenges of dog ownership is living up to the standards our dogs set for us. If we were everything that our dogs seem to think we are, we'd be a much better species.

Try to live up to your dog's expectations of you. He expects you to be kind to him, to take care of his needs, and to be there for him Be a stable presence for your dog. You know he'll return the favor many times over.

4 He's a Dog!

When we integrate our dogs into our family, we have a tendency to treat them like human family members and to expect that they'll behave accordingly. The trouble is, there are fundamental differences between dogs and humans. We do our dogs a disservice when we think of them as little people in fur coats.

I'm as guilty of this as anybody. Kramer and Scout are a large part of our little family. They communicate their needs and desires so well. They seem to understand what we tell them, and I sometimes fall into the trap of expecting them to conform to human standards of behavior.

DON'T PLACE UNREALISTIC EXPECTATIONS ON YOUR PET

During the summer garbage season in the park, Scout reminds me on a daily basis that she's a dog. Despite my asking her not to, she persists in picking up and eating chicken bones, soiled napkins, and whatever she can get her mouth on. In most other situations, she drops things when I ask her to, but when it's trash, she gets a determined look in her eye, and we have a battle of wills that typically involves my prying open her mouth and extracting the offending item. I get angry. But then I remind myself that she's a dog, doing what dogs do. I can't expect her not to do things that are hardwired into her.

Understand a Dog's Nature

In her book *The Culture Clash,* Jean Donaldson writes about the conflict between human expectations of dogs and what dogs really are. They're out to please themselves, she writes. They're scavengers. They're programmed to chase things that run.

A comparison of some of the things Donaldson says dogs are and aren't can be useful in figuring out what makes your dog tick. Since they are more interested in pleasing themselves than pleasing you, for example, it's more efficient to train with food rewards than merely with praise.

> **▼ POOCH POINTER ▼**
>
> *According to Jean Donaldson, dogs are:*
> - *self-interested*
> - *predators*
> - *highly social*
> - *scavengers*
> - *amoral (they don't assign moral value to things)*
>
> *Dogs aren't:*
> - *abstract thinkers*
> - *eager to please*
> - *moral*
> - *spiteful*
> - *Lassie*

While Donaldson's perspective is valuable, it seems to boil dogs down to a series of responses, ignoring the fact that they are emotional, thinking creatures. I recognize that my dogs are fully formed beings, but I find it useful to remind myself that they're responding to life as dogs, not as humans. I have to admit that I relate to them so much that sometimes I forget they're not human.

Understanding what dogs are (and aren't) helps us to work with them. They are motivated by food and access to fun and games. They seek to please themselves, not the handler. Once we accept that, we can train accordingly. Donaldson asserts (as do most of the trainers I interviewed for this book) that dogs respond better to positive reinforcement than to punishment (see chapter 5). By using positive reinforcement, you work with your dog's natural tendency to do things to please herself rather than asking her to refrain from doing things to avoid punishment. Reward the good behavior and ignore the bad. Rather than expecting mere praise to be sufficient, give your dog a payday for performing the behaviors you want. Not only is positive reinforcement a more effective way to train, but it's also more fun for both of you.

Don't Assume Knowledge

Another way we can be unfair to our dogs is when we believe they know something, like a command (or a cue, as positive trainers call it), but are just being stubborn by not doing it.

Dogs don't generalize well. If your dog breaks his stay—one that was so solid in the house—when you try it at the park, he isn't being stubborn or willful. A stay in the house just isn't the same to him as a stay at the park. Go back a few steps when you're in the park, and ask for a shorter stay, or one where you're closer to him. Or both.

The repetition in a variety of settings helps the dog truly grasp the cue. "If your dog doesn't do it, it's because your dog doesn't know it," says Becky Schultz, a dog trainer in Shorewood, Minnesota. "When in doubt, assume your dog doesn't know the behavior. It takes a lot of repetitions."

Schultz says her clients tend to think that if they teach their dog a behavior, the dog will know it after only a few repetitions. "They don't understand that dogs learn differently from the way we do."

If your dog refuses a request you think he understands, pause, and think about why he might not really understand. Maybe the context is different, or perhaps you're motivating him differently. My dogs sit readily if I stand in front of them in the living room, with the smell of a treat wafting around me. Usually, they sit before I ask them to. But if they're just standing around in the bedroom, and I ask them to sit for no apparent reason, they might blink at me and pause before actually complying. They're not being stubborn. They're taking the time to think, "What's in it for me?"

Holding Dogs to a Higher Standard

Sometimes it seems that people expect their dogs to exceed human standards of behavior. When you have a good dog, you expect him to be good 100 percent of the time. That's not fair. Humans certainly aren't good 100 percent of the time.

Don't ask your dog to put up with everything. For example, don't let a child get in your dog's face, and don't force your dog to interact with someone she's trying to get away from.

"It amazes me that we expect our animals to be more tolerant and have more self-control in life than we have," says dog trainer Sarah Wilson, coauthor with Brian Kilcommons of *Good Owners, Great Dogs* and *Childproofing Your Dog.*

We leave all sorts of temptations out for the four-legged scavengers who share our lives. "It is not kind to leave things where your dog can get them," says Schultz. She would no sooner leave a tasty tidbit out on the coffee table, where her dogs could get them, than she would leave cookies on the counter with her six-year-old daughter around. "We often expect more of our dogs than we do of a six-year-old," she says. Indeed it seems we forgive a lot more of a small child than we do of dogs.

The Dark Side of Treating Dogs Like Humans

"One of the major causes of death in dogs is people anthropomorphizing," Schultz says. Dog owners misunderstand canine nature, set impossible standards for dogs, and then have them euthanized because of behavioral problems. "We expect them to understand things that they don't," she says.

For example, people expect dogs to immediately grasp the concept that they should go to the bathroom outdoors rather than in the house. "If you put a chicken in your living room, you'd expect it to poop." Dogs need to be taught, with patience, about good manners in human society, which can differ so much from canine society. Among canines, for instance, butt sniffing is expected, and poop eating is acceptable.

Dogs chew, bite, bark, and poop. These are innate canine behaviors. Such behaviors also get dogs put to sleep, says Schultz. "Some people like the idea of

▼ POOCH POINTER ▼

SMALL DOGS ARE STILL DOGS

Toy dogs, in particular, says Schultz, are often treated as if they're not actually dogs. But they're not stuffed toys; they are living, breathing dogs, with canine nature and needs. It's not fair to deprive your small dog of exercise, a social life with other canines, and training—things people tend to routinely provide to larger dogs.

having a dog, but they don't have tolerance for how their dogs act. They don't understand that they are dogs, and that's what dogs do."

If you stop expecting your dog to act like a human, you can start enjoying her as a dog. Canines and humans have lived together for thousands of years, but they're separate and unique species. Give your dog credit for being who she is. After all, she loves you for who you are, flaws and all.

5 Reward, Don't Punish

Most humans' motivation to go to work every day is the paycheck they receive every other week. So why are so many people opposed to paying their dogs to do the things they want them to do? Traditional training is about telling dogs what not to do rather than rewarding them for doing the right thing. Folks who reject the use of food treats insist that praise is reward enough. They seem to prefer the idea that their dog chooses not to misbehave out of fear of the consequences rather than choosing to behave well because they desire the reward.

DON'T USE PHYSICAL CORRECTIONS WITH YOUR DOG

Training by punishment is how dog trainers have worked for generations. Some of the most popular books on dog training still promote the method of "correcting" your dog by jerking on his chain collar; they want you to show him that you're the boss (the "alpha" dog) by physically rolling him onto his back and holding him there until he submits to your will.

This is no fun, and I can almost guarantee it's no fun for your dog. Moreover, it's dangerous. If you put your dog in an alpha roll, you're giving him a great opportunity to bite you in the face.

Punishment Is Less Effective Than You Think

Modern, progressive methods of dog training advise rewarding desirable behavior and ignoring that which is undesirable. Dogs are inherently self-involved. They don't do things to please you, says Jean Donaldson in her book *The Culture Clash*; they're out to please themselves. If they can get you to reward them for their actions, they're likely to repeat them. Why not work *with* this inclination rather than trying to tell your dog what not to do? There's nothing wrong with rewarding good behavior.

One of the problems with punishment as a training method is that it must be used absolutely consistently in order for it to work, says Ian Dunbar, who also wrote *Dog Behavior: An Owner's Guide to a Happy Healthy Pet.* That's nearly impossible for people to do. We're only human, after all. An owner will miss punishing a behavior at least once, and that's when the lightbulb goes on inside the dog's head, and he realizes that he can sometimes get away with bad behavior.

"You need to be a very, very good dog trainer to be able to use punishment," says Dunbar. "It is so difficult, and there are so many screwups."

Positive reinforcement, on the other hand, works best when it's on a variable schedule of reinforcement. If you reward only occasionally, it's more exciting to the dog, and the good behavior is strengthened. Trainers liken it to a slot machine. We keep putting our coins in, hoping for a big payoff. Part of the excitement is not knowing when the payoff will come. (This is one reason why it's a good idea to use a variety of rewards with dogs, and to have a jackpot reward for excellent behavior.)

Just as we're inconsistent with punishment, we sometimes miss rewarding a desirable behavior. But unlike punishment, that works to our advantage. By naturally being inconsistent, we unwittingly put the behavior on a variable schedule of reinforcement and, thus, strengthen the behavior. This is one case where being fallible actually works in your favor!

Punishment Has Side Effects

"Even when punishment training has been apparently effective in resolving simple behavioral problems, it invariably shakes the dog's confidence and undermines the trusting relationship between trainer and animal, which ultimately destroys the dog's temperament," writes Andrea Arden in *Dog-Friendly Dog Training*. Your dog may do what you ask, but he'll probably learn to dislike training, and heaven knows, you don't want him to dislike the trainer. In that case, writes Arden, "the owner has won the battle but lost the war."

Arden knows from whence she speaks. Like most trainers, she once used traditional training techniques that relied on physical corrections. She's a convert to positive training, as her book amply illustrates. Any aversive techniques she uses are nonphysical.

Dogs that are trained with physical corrections frequently become desensitized to the correction, which makes the trainer resort to increasingly harsh corrections.

I experienced this firsthand with Kramer, whose traditional training program involved leash corrections, scruff shakes, and even alpha rolls. I hated every second of it. I watched the corrections become progressively less effective.

Since switching to more positive methods, corrections are hardly necessary, and when I do use them, they're not nearly as harsh as they once were. (Of course, it helps that I'm now working with an eight-year-old dog rather than an unruly one-year-old.)

Manage Bad Behavior

If your dog has some bad habits you're having trouble getting him to stop, you can try to manage, rather than solve, the problem. "If you can't get the behavior you want through training, then you really need management," says Deborah Manheim, a dog trainer in Brooklyn, New York.

For example, if your dog is a counter-surfer, don't leave stuff on the counter for him to get. If she steals laundry, put away the laundry. If your dog is aggressive, muzzle him. If she jumps on the bed when you're not home (and you don't want her there), close the bedroom door. These are all management techniques.

The idea is to not give the dog a chance to misbehave. If you start this as soon as you get your dog, before he learns the unwanted behavior, you're a step ahead of the game. "If you manage your dog 100 percent, you don't need training," Manheim says.

Of course, it's hard to manage anything all the time. So training is a good idea. Sometimes you can combine the two. For example, if your dog chews up your stuff when you're not home, you can manage the problem by crating him, or by putting him in a long-term confinement area. At the same time, you can train him while he's in the crate. If you always give him a delicious chew toy—something that is safe for him to chew when you're not at home, like a stuffed Kong—you're training him to have a good chewing habit. You're also training him to enjoy quiet time. After a while, you may well be able to leave him loose in the house to chew on sanctioned toys and to enjoy quiet time. That way you won't face the unpleasant experience of discovering chewed-up clothing and furniture.

> **▼ POOCH POINTER ▼**
>
> **TECHNIQUES FOR MANAGING BAD BEHAVIOR**
>
> *Sometimes it's easier to manage a problem behavior —and prevent it from occurring—rather than to solve the problem. Good management techniques include:*
>
> - *removing temptations*
> - *confining your dog*
> - *exercising your dog*
> - *controlling your dog by using a leash*
> - *muzzling your aggressive dog*

All of us manage our dogs all of the time, whether we realize it or not. When we use a leash, we're managing. Rather than training the dog to walk off-leash at a perfect, reliable heel, we leash him to keep him safe. (I'm not suggesting that it's better to train an off-leash heel—no dog is reliable enough to walk down city streets off-leash.) We're also managing our dog when we put him out in the fenced yard rather than train him to stay in the yard (another good idea).

One management tool, which Manheim declares "the most important," is exercise. Use it! (See chapter 9 for more information on the importance of exercise.) By tiring out your dog, you keep him out of all sorts of trouble.

Management allows you to keep your dog safe and to prevent her from learning undesirable behaviors. It takes some creativity, but it sure beats constantly yelling at your dog, and it makes training a lot easier.

Teach Self-Control

"Dogs naturally tend to act in the moment," says Arden. "What we want from pets is for them to take a breath, and think." Trouble is, that's not normal dog behavior. But some simple exercises can be done with your dog to help him learn some self-control. One Arden described—and she credits dog trainer Leslie Nelson for showing it to her—is to put the dog on-leash. Put something delicious on the ground just out of the dog's reach. When he stops straining at the leash to get it, reward him (either with the stuff that was on the ground, or something from your hand). "The dog learns to relax and to not charge for the food," Arden says. Nelson uses the same exercise to teach a stay.

Reward Rather Than Punish

When I'm in the park, I frequently see dogs who are driving their owners nuts, yet the owners sometimes refuse my offer of help to get their dog to focus on a treat. One particular man has a sweet pit bull who has the bad habit of jumping up and grabbing her leash, trying for a game of tug-of-war when it's time to leash up and go home.

I know this dog is motivated by treats. I always have some with me (and she always tries to mooch one), so sometimes I'll ask if I can offer her a treat in exchange for a sit—this calms her so he can put on her leash and walk home. The owner always refuses, claiming that she shouldn't need a treat to behave correctly. Instead, he physically threatens his dog by putting his fist over her head and shaking it until she sits. It puzzles me why he prefers this method to rewarding her with a treat for sitting.

The underlying principle of positive training is to reward good behavior and ignore bad behavior. If your dog is doing something wrong, ask him to do something incompatible with the bad behavior, something you can reward. Then reward him for it. For example, if he jumps on you, silently turn your back to him (withdrawing your attention), then turn around, and ask him to sit (a behavior incompatible with jumping up). Reward him for sitting.

People seem to believe that dogs should work to please their humans. Dogs are dogs, and they do things to please themselves. So why not make it easy on yourself, and make good things happen to your dog when she does what you want her to?

6 You're the Center of His Universe

Like children, dogs thrive on love and attention. Imagine giving birth to a child and then rarely interacting with him. You would end up with a lonely, angry child forced to devise ways to amuse himself. Is that the kind of dog you want?

▸ DON'T LEAVE YOUR DOG ALONE DAY AND NIGHT ◂

Most dogs are left alone while their owners go to work. It is a lucky few that go to work with them. Others, like my dogs, are fortunate enough to have a mom or dad who works from home. But most spend their days alone.

Your coming home from work is one of the highlights of your dog's day. But if you come home, let your dog out, feed her, and then go right back out again to have fun, you are putting your dog on an emotional roller coaster. What she wants, more than anything, is to spend time with you.

The wonderful thing about dogs is that they're content to simply be in the presence of their humans. You can watch TV, pay the bills, even talk on the phone, and as long as you're in the same room, or within earshot, your dog will most likely be happy—if she's getting sufficient exercise. If your pet is insufficiently exercised, she might bug you when you're home with her. She'll bring you her toys, maybe bark at you, even do something naughty in a bid to get your attention.

Of course, your dog would prefer some intense interaction with you—play, massages, going somewhere, or just talking. But just having you around fulfills a real need for companionship.

Dogs Are Social Creatures

Wolves live in packs. To dogs, who evolved from wolves, the pack is still very important. They don't care that their pack is human; they just want to be with it. If your dog spends much of his time outdoors, I encourage you to bring him inside. (See chapter 19 for more information on why your dog should live indoors.) But even if he's inside, your dog won't be happy if he's often alone.

If you work long hours, maybe a dog isn't the right pet for you. If you find yourself in a position where you've begun working additional hours, think about some alternate ways for your dog to spend the day.

If your dog has a good friend, perhaps you could explore the possibility of their spending the day together. That's ideal if the canine friend happens to have a stay-at-home owner.

If staying with a friend isn't a possibility, look into doggie day care. In many cities, dogs are taken to a day-care facility where, under close supervision, they're allowed to play with other canines. For working owners of young, energetic dogs, day care can make a world of difference. Pick up your dog at the end of the day, and he's already tuckered out. You're glad to see one another, but you can enjoy quiet time together. If your dog were home alone all day, he'd spend the day snoozing and be ready for action upon your return.

Day care is also helpful for dogs with separation anxiety. When her rescue cocker spaniel, Barney, began whining and barking all day (as reported by intolerant neighbors), Linda Weiss of East Lansing, Michigan, started taking Barney to day care at her vet's office. "Day care has been a godsend in several ways," Weiss says. "It has allowed us to stay in our residence. It has desensitized Barney to our leaving, and it has also helped to socialize him with other people and other dogs. It has been such a relief to know that Barney isn't all alone and miserable, and instead is in a safe, caring environment."

In Boston, a day-care service offered by a company called the Common Dog actually sends a school bus around to pick up the dogs (the animals are securely belted into the seats) and take them to day care. At the end of the day, the bus brings them home.

Another option is a professional dog walker. Dog walking is a big business in New York City, where people commonly work long hours and have long commutes. The dog walker comes in once or twice during the day to take the pet for a walk or to the dog run. Sometimes walkers walk the dogs in groups, giving them an instant social life.

One of the interesting side effects of such arrangements is that your dog ends up with a life you don't know about. A friend who used a dog walker would take her dog for walks and be surprised when people she'd never seen before greeted Kate by name. Occasionally, Kate would drag her up to the front door of houses my friend had never visited before.

But You're the Important One

All these arrangements can be beneficial to dogs who spend their days alone. But they don't substitute for actually spending time with you, the center of your dog's universe. Every day, you should fit in some quality time with your dog, where the two of you can converse, snuggle, and just enjoy being together. Try to spend a little time focusing your attention on your dog rather than patting her absently while you watch TV. Giving her a gentle rub all over will alert you to any lumps or bumps (see chapter 16). Regular brushing or combing will also bring you together and keep your dog healthier (see chapter 18).

My husband, Barry, enjoys daily time with Kramer and Scout, when he just lies on the floor with them (separately), strokes them, and talks quietly to them. I don't know what he's telling them, but they all seem to enjoy it.

Get Out and About Together

The daily, indoor time is important for building and fostering the bond between you and your dog, but it can also be fun to spend time outside with her. There are many activities in which you can include your dog.

If you're able to take your dog with you, he'll need to be well behaved (see chapter 12 for more on the importance of training), and you'll need to be well behaved, too (see chapter 8 for some rules you need to follow to ensure that you and your dog are welcome in public). But if your dog is friendly with people, friendly with dogs, and is not so high-strung that he is stressed out among new people, consider some of the following activities:

Car Trips

Most dogs love riding in the car, and they can be great company, even if no other humans are present. Scout would be the perfect driving companion if only she had thumbs so she could share the driving.(Kramer is hyperstimulated in the car and is actually somewhat of a trial to drive with, so he doesn't get to take as many car trips.)

Sixty-seven percent of pet owners surveyed by the American Animal Hospital Association in 1998 said they've traveled with their pets. Ninety-nine percent of those said they travel by car. It's a fun and easy way to spend time with your animal.

You don't have to limit yourself to day trips. Many hotels and motels accept dogs. It's wise to plan ahead, so that you don't find yourself in a situation where you and your dog don't have a place to stay. Leaving your dog in the car is not an option: It's too dangerous. If your car were stolen (and I've heard of this happening to dog owners), you'd never forgive yourself. God forbid your dog should accidentally put the car out of gear, and it rolled away. Besides, parked cars aren't climate-controlled.

A number of guides provides information on accommodations for dog lovers seeking to travel with their canine buddies. They include:

- *Canine Adventures: Fun Things To Do With Your Dog* by Cynthia D. Miller
- *On the Road Again with Man's Best Friend (United States)* by Dawn and Robert Habgood. (Regional editions are also available.)
- *Take Your Pet Along* by Heather MacLean Walters
- *Take Your Pet Too! Fun Things to Do!* by Heather MacLean Walters
- *Vacationing with your Pet* by Eileen Barish

In addition, several searchable Web sites can help you not only to plan a trip with your dog but also to find a place to stay. Check out www.petswelcome.com, www.traveldog.com, and www.petvacations.com.

For confirmed travelers who enjoy canine companionship, the newsletter "DogGone" (see Recommended Reading) provides reviews of dog-welcome vacation destinations, as well as travel tips.

Activities and Competitions

Competitions sponsored by the American Kennel Club (AKC) are open to AKC-registered purebred dogs. AKC activities run the gamut, including field trials and agility skills, obedience, conformation, and more. In addition, individual sports have organizations that offer competitions that are open to both purebred and mixed-breed dogs. For example, the North American Dog Agility Council offers agility competitions in which dogs, directed by their handler, run at high speeds through obstacle courses.

Competing with your dog in a dog-related sport is an ideal way to spend time with him. It's dog-focused and designed for dogs. Not all canines enjoy competitions, but there are so many different activities that a motivated owner could doubtless find one that suits both dog and human. Your best bet is to take training classes for most of these events before deciding to compete. (See chapter 9 for more information on various dog activities.)

▼ POOCH POINTER ▼

CANINE SPORTS AND ACTIVITIES

- *agility*
- *camping*
- *conformation (dog shows)*
- *dog park visits*
- *field trials*
- *flyball*
- *freestyle*
- *Frisbee*
- *hiking*
- *herding*
- *obedience competitions*

Dog Parks

Dog parks—areas where dogs are allowed to run and play off-leash—can be a boon to your dog's social life (and your own). They also provide a marvelous opportunity for exercise. Many dog parks, or "dog runs," are fenced areas. If your dog tends to bolt, you'll want to seek a fenced park. Some parks are unfenced but large. If your dog consistently comes when called, such a park can provide vast, open space in which he can run and play with other dogs. We go to a park like this nearly every day—I don't know how we'd survive city life without it.

At dog parks, you have the chance to meet other dedicated dog owners, which is great. But your priority should be your dog. Keep your eye on her, know her signals, and call her to you if it looks like she might not be getting along with another dog. Always keep her within sight. Avoid the temptation to get lost in conversation. Instead, be an attentive guardian to your dog.

Dog Camps

What could be more heavenly for you and your dog than to spend a week together focusing on dog-related activities? That's what you can do at several camps around the country. Each offers athletic activities like agility and flyball, as well as outdoor fun and silly contests. Kramer and I attended Camp Gone to the Dogs in Vermont in 1998 and had a great time. Camp offered an extraordinary environment in which dogs always come first. In addition to fun activities, this camp also offers lectures and other opportunities for dog owners to keep learning about how best to provide stewardship for their dogs. (See chapter 21 for more on the importance of continuing to learn and to broaden your horizons as your dog grows up.) The Resources section offers names and addresses of dog camps around the country.

▼ POOCH POINTER ▼

SAFETY CONSIDERATIONS

When you take your dog places, safety should be your number one priority. Always bring plenty of fresh water. Don't leave your animal unattended in the car, particularly in hot or cold weather. Your dog should wear an ID tag with your cellular phone number on it (and keep your cell phone with you). Or you can use a paper key tag and Sharpie permanent marker to make a temporary ID tag that includes the telephone number of your hotel and an emergency backup number. Keep your dog on-leash in unfamiliar places, particularly roadside rest areas. The idea of losing a dog away from home is too awful to think about.

Hiking

Taking your dog along with you when you go hiking and backpacking can enhance your enjoyment of the great outdoors. For longer outings, your dog can even be outfitted with a backpack and carry his own supplies. Make sure that your dog is physically fit enough to handle unfamiliar terrain and potentially longer stretches of exercise than he might be accustomed to. A nature hike will be more strenuous than a walk taken on the city sidewalk. Take along plenty of water for your dog. You can bring a collapsible nylon water bowl, a pet canteen, or you can teach your dog to drink right out of the bottle.

Time Together Is Worth the Effort

If you participate in activities your dog can also enjoy, you have a win-win situation. You and your dog can be together on weekends, and you can still get out. Don't take your dog along if it means that he'll spend all his time in a car or motel room. As we've noted, leaving your dog in the car isn't safe, and he's more alone in the unfamiliar setting of a motel room without you than he is at home.

If you're having trouble settling on an activity to share with your dog, the Web site www.dog-play.com offers detailed information on almost every type of dog-related activity. Browse through it, and you might come up with some new ideas.

Cynthia Miller's book *Canine Adventures: Fun Things To Do With Your Dog* is a marvelous resource. It not only describes a wide variety of activities, but it also discusses in detail getting your dog into good physical condition so that she can safely participate in the activities.

Whenever you take your dog with you, remember that you're an ambassador for all dog owners. It's amazing what ill will a single irresponsible dog person can create for all dogs. Always clean up after your dog and leave no indication that the two of you were there. Dogs would be welcome in more places if more dog owners acted responsibly. Do your part to make sure that the places you visit with your dog continue to welcome canine travelers.

7 Socialize, Socialize, Socialize

You want a happy, well-adjusted dog, one who gets along with not only family members and pets but also with visitors, strangers, and other animals. If your dog gets along well with others, you'll take him with you more places, you can spend more time with him, and his life will be a lot more interesting. It's worth the effort.

▸ DON'T ISOLATE YOUR DOG ◂

I'll never forget the day I saw an adorable pit bull puppy on-leash at a grocery store parking lot in St. Louis. The tiny puppy was about three months old and cute as a button. I eagerly asked the owner permission to pet him. To my surprise, the woman said no. "I don't allow anyone to handle him but me. I want him to be a guard dog." I was so dumbfounded and upset by her reply that words failed me.

Now I wish I had pointed out to her that allowing her puppy to interact with a variety of people would not make him any less protective. Denying him the opportunity to be comfortable around strangers would not only make him less happy but would also make him more likely to bite someone who was not a threat. A pit bull (or any dog) who bites is not a welcome member of society.

"It is an absolute catastrophe if a dog isn't socialized to people," says Ian Dunbar. He counts not socializing their dog among the biggest mistakes a dog owner can make. If a dog is not socialized during his early puppy months, he will never be what he could have been, he says. A poorly socialized dog will live an anxious life, afraid of people. "It's not fair to the dog," Dunbar declares.

Socializing Puppies

If you're contemplating getting a puppy, or have just brought one home, make socializing her your number one priority. "The earlier you start socialization, the stronger the foundation is," says Pat Miller.

Dunbar outlines a program for exposing your puppy to a variety of people during his third month (from the time he's eight weeks old until he is three months). Your puppy should meet at least one hundred people during that month. It's not as hard as it sounds, Dunbar says, and it can do wonders for *your* social life.

Those hundred people should include men, women, and children, and those strangers should actually spend some time training the puppy. Dunbar describes his socialization program in detail in *How to Teach a New Dog Old Tricks*, but the highlights include:

Twice a week, invite a group of six men to your house for the purposes of socializing and training your puppy. Offer refreshments, but tell them that the goodies don't arrive until after they've practiced these four behaviors with your little puppy: come, sit, lie down, and roll over. They should hand-feed the puppy his supper, using pieces of food to get him to come when called and to lure him into a sit, down, and even roll over.

After your puppy has gotten the hang of it over the course of the month (which he will after all this repetition), your guests should put the food out of sight and use hand signals (pantomiming the lure that your puppy's been watching). When the puppy performs, out comes the reward.

When your puppy has that down, use the treats as a distraction. One person should hold the food while another gives him a command. The person with the food then goes over to the puppy with a reward.

In addition to two groups of six men per week, invite two groups of six women, and have them perform the same activities with your puppy. You'll also need to involve kids—but only one at a time. After all the practice your puppy has under his belt, it should be easy for him to perform these tricks at a child's request.

The beauty of this system is that you're basically getting other people to train your puppy for you, says Dunbar. On top of that, your puppy is being exposed to lots of strangers, all of whom are providing a positive experience. The puppy is willingly sitting, lying down, and rolling over for these folks, proving that he's comfortable with them.

Rolling over is particularly important because it gets the puppy to willingly assume a position of deference, even for a stranger or a child. It's also a handy command to use when you need to examine your dog's undercarriage.

If your puppy is exposed to a hundred strangers in this way for that important third month, he will be happy and comfortable—and well behaved—around strangers for the rest of his life.

If the idea of inviting one hundred people into your home is a little daunting, try fifty, or twelve. The more people your puppy is exposed to, the better, but any number is better than none.

If circumstances prevent you from bringing people in, you can take your puppy out. Common wisdom suggests that you need to protect your puppy from disease before he's vaccinated, but you can get around that by holding him and not letting his feet touch the ground, says Andrea Arden. Go to the park, hold your puppy in your lap, and look friendly. People are almost guaranteed to flock to the dog. Hand them treats to give your puppy and ask them to gently pet the little dog.

Having a puppy party at your home is preferable, says Arden, but at least the dog is becoming accustomed to people and starting to like them even more because they're giving him treats. "Whatever you do, don't keep your dog in social isolation," Arden warns. "Anything you can do to avoid that is a step in the right direction."

After this month is up, you must continue the socialization process. Since your puppy is comfortable with the world (and since you have all these friends you've had occasion to spend time with lately), take your puppy out on visits and errands. Keep up his socialization so it doesn't slip.

Socializing Adult Dogs

What if your dog is no longer a puppy? What if you didn't socialize her as a puppy or if you got her as an adult and she doesn't seem well-socialized?

All is not lost. If your dog is generally confident, you may be able to turn her around. If she's timid, you probably won't be able to transform her into a bold and confident dog. But you can try to make her more comfortable with her surroundings.

Dunbar's "puppy party" method is especially suited for puppies in their critical formative weeks, when they can't be taken out of the house until their immunity to common diseases is developed. It's easier to get an adult dog out to meet people and other dogs. However, pay close attention to her signals, and give her only as much exposure to others as she can handle.

▼ POOCH POINTER ▼

THE BENEFITS OF OWNING A WELL-SOCIALIZED DOG ARE:

- ***You can take her anywhere.***
- ***She's confident and comfortable in all situations.***
- ***You're more comfortable when your dog is comfortable.***
- ***You don't have to worry that your dog will hurt someone—human or canine.***
- ***You can walk down the street with your dog and encounter anyone.***

If your dog has developed fears of specific things, you can start a program of counterconditioning and desensitization, says Pat Miller, by providing her with a lot of positive exposure to the things that scare her. If your dog is afraid of traffic, for instance, take her to an area where she can be near lots of cars, but not so close that she completely freaks out. As cars pass, give her lots and lots of treats. "Treats should rain from the sky," Miller says.

It doesn't matter what your dog's doing. She may be barking and lunging at the cars, but keep giving her the treats. "You are not giving her a single treat, you are flooding her with treats," says Miller. "Giving a single treat is rewarding the undesirable behavior, which can be a big mistake." By flooding her with treats, you're trying to change her association with the object of her fear, in this case passing cars. You want your dog to think of traffic not as something scary but rather as the thing that makes you give her delicious treats.

Make sure the treat is something wonderful, and use it for this situation only.

This approach is called classical conditioning. You can expect some frowns of disapproval from strangers as they watch you reward what looks like bad behavior. These strangers would probably rather see you yelling at your dog for misbehaving. "Be ready to resist that whole social approval for punishing a behavior," Miller says.

If you have a fearful dog on your hands, seek professional help in overcoming his fears. Look for someone who employs classical conditioning or other positive methods.

Another great source of information on this method is Jean Donaldson's book *The Culture Clash*, as well as her follow-up book, *Dogs Are from Neptune.* In these books, Donaldson refers to "an open bar" rather than "treats raining from the sky." But it's the same concept.

Dog-Dog Socialization

Ian Dunbar thinks it's important to make sure your puppy is more comfortable around people than other dogs. The consequences for a dog who is nasty to people are more severe than for a dog who is nasty to other dogs. Many dogs do not lead lives where they're exposed to a lot of other dogs.

But speaking as someone whose dogs come into contact with a lot of other dogs, life is a lot more pleasant if your dog is socialized to other dogs. Having a dog-friendly dog allows you to take him to more places, and also allows you to participate in doggie events, like dog walks and pet expos.

Again, it makes life a lot more pleasant for your dog. If he is fearful and/or aggressive with other dogs, he won't have much of a social life. Being around other dogs can be fun for dogs, so don't let your canine miss out on this part of life.

If you have a puppy, once your vet tells you he can be around other dogs without risk of getting any diseases, enroll him in puppy kindergarten. Most puppy classes allow social time for the "youngsters."

If puppy kindergarten isn't available (or even if it is), you can arrange some play dates for your puppy. Try to give him the opportunity to play with a variety of gentle dogs—different sizes, ages, colors, builds. When your puppy is playing, try not to be overprotective. Puppies yelp to tell other dogs that they've had enough or that they're frightened. Your puppy probably doesn't need you to run interference for him. Try to give the other dog the opportunity to back off. They'll probably recommence their play.

Our dogs are tuned in to us. If you're nervous about another dog, yours will sense it and be nervous and defensive—and perhaps protective of you. Remain calm, relaxed, and friendly when meeting new dogs. "Act the way you want your dog to act," says dog trainer Sarah Wilson.

As your puppy grows up and becomes an unruly adolescent, he may be less angelic around other dogs. Don't use that as a reason to isolate him. Kelly Skiptunas of Lancaster, Pennsylvania, did just that when her rottweiler, Ruger, hit the teenage rebellion stage. "When he got to the age of about ten months, he went berserk," she recalls, "growling, lunging, and barking at other dogs." Skiptunas mistakenly thought that if she kept him away from other people and other animals, he would calm down on his own. "It didn't happen," she says.

So she started a desensitization program, beginning about a hundred yards away from situations that might set him off. "We put him in down or sit stays with attention for a few seconds, and treats and praise. We worked up to a few minutes at a time as the weeks passed." Eventually, Ruger calmed down when he realized he could also get attention by being good, says Skiptunas. "He began to accept new situations at closer and closer range without lunging." Ruger regained his composure and is now even able to hold his cool at a dog show.

Socializing your dog is one of the most important things you can do for him. It will make him more comfortable around people and other dogs, which is more fun for him. It will also make you more comfortable. Every bit of effort you put into this socialization process is repaid many times over.

8 Make Your Dog Welcome in Public

As a dog owner, I hate it when I see a beautiful, fenced-in park with a "No Dogs Allowed" sign attached to the fence. My response is always "my dogs aren't going to do any harm. I clean up after them. Why shouldn't we be able to use the park?" But in my heart, I know the answer. It's because dog owners frequently use parks irresponsibly. They let their dogs trample the landscaping, or they allow them to run up to people and scare them. Of course, they also commit the cardinal sin of dog ownership: not cleaning up after their dogs.

DON'T FORGET YOUR OWN MANNERS

Even devoted dog owners are disgusted when they see a pile of dog feces. Or worse, when they step in it. For the life of me, I can't understand why some dog owners feel cleaning up after their dogs is not their responsibility. There must be a "it's biodegradable, it'll go away on its own" mind-set at work. But in most urban landscapes, it's seen by many people before it biodegrades. Such carelessness gives all dog owners a bad name.

Not picking up dog feces is just one way in which irresponsible owners practice bad manners and make dogs unwelcome. If more dog owners (and their dogs) behaved properly, dogs would be welcome in more places. Americans who visit Europe often marvel at the access dogs have to public places. I don't know if it's because European dogs are better trained or better tolerated. But I suspect it's a combination of the two.

If you'd like to see your dog welcome in more places, you can do your part by practicing good manners.

Clean Up After Your Dog

There's no excuse not to pick up your dog's poop. It's easy, it's the right thing to do, and it's a public health hazard not to. I use the plastic-bag method. I recycle plastic produce or grocery bags, always making sure to have a supply on hand when I'm out with the dogs. When one of them makes a deposit, I simply put my hand in the bag, grab the poop, turn the bag inside out—so that the poop's inside—and tie the top. Then I put it in a public trash can, or take it home to my own outdoor trash container.

Some people prefer to carry a pooper scooper, which (I guess) keeps them farther from the poop. In New York City, many people use newspapers to clean up after their dogs, sometimes sliding the newspaper under their dog's butt to catch the deposit. The dog-supply catalogs have other devices you can try. It doesn't matter how you clean it up, just do it!

Remember that diseases are carried in feces, so don't let your dog sniff or (ugh) eat any deposits that canines who have left behind with ill-mannered owners.

Teach Your Dog Manners

When you're out on the street, don't let your dog run up to strangers. Being greeted by a strange dog can frighten people. Keep your dog at your side when you pass a person on the sidewalk. I use treats to keep my dogs focused on me.

If your dog tends to jump up on people, by all means put a stop to that practice. (See chapter 12 for more benefits of training.) Your dog should also know how to sit nicely (and stay put) when asked. If you allow your dog to greet a person, he should do it politely. (While crotch sniffing makes perfect sense to him, most humans find it embarrassing.)

In addition to respecting other people, respect other dogs. Don't let your dog rush up to another dog who is on-leash. Leashes can make some dogs defensive, and if they can't run away from the object of their fear, they frequently lash out. Always ask the other dog's owner for permission before allowing your dog to greet another one.

Control Your Dog

You should have control of your dog when you're out in public together. If you're out on the street, it's unsafe and unwise for her to be off-leash. Chances are, it's also illegal. Even if you feel your dog is perfectly trained, and you trust that she won't run off or bolt into the street, you're taking a big risk by walking her off-leash on a city sidewalk. First of all, other people don't know she's perfectly trained, and they might well be scared. You never know when she might surprise you and run after the ultimate temptation—like a squirrel or cat—and dart into the street. It only takes a moment of weakness on your dog's part to have a truly tragic result.

Speaking of leashes, teach your dog to walk on a loose leash. You really can't control her well if she's straining at the end of the leash. Some types of equipment, like a head harness or prong collar, can help stem a pulling habit (see chapter 10 for a discussion of equipment), but it's preferable to train you dog to walk on a loose leash rather than rely on a piece of equipment.

A positive dog trainer can teach you methods that use food rewards and perhaps a clicker rather than punishment. It's not always easy (depending on your dog), but it's worth the effort. It can turn a walk into a pleasure rather than a chore.

If your dog is legally allowed off-leash, like in an off-leash park or out in the country, he should be under voice control. A dog who doesn't come when called needs more training before he's allowed off-leash. One of the most upsetting sights in our large off-leash (and unfenced) park is the dog owner frantically calling her dog's name, with the dog nowhere in sight.

Every time I have my dogs at the off-leash park, we make a game of coming when called. While they're otherwise occupied, I wander perhaps 20 feet away, then call them. They come running, because they know there's a tasty morsel waiting. I realize that some dogs are easier to train than others, but I encourage you to practice calling yours regularly (and rewarding him for coming) rather than just in urgent situations.

Be Aware of Your Surroundings

No matter how courteous you are with your dogs, other users of the sidewalk and parks are often less courteous. Joggers, bicyclists, and in-line skaters can (and do) race up behind you when you're walking your dog, without announcing their approach. From a dog's perspective, that's an invitation to give chase. If you don't know they're coming, you'll find out when your dog lunges after them, and you feel like your arm's being pulled out of its socket. Worse, your dog could pull the leash out of your hand and actually give chase.

When I'm walking Kramer and Scout on the street, particularly when we're near the park, I keep my antennae out for these ill-mannered people, fearing that my dogs will be as startled as I, and lunge in fear. I wouldn't blame my dogs for doing that—but I'm certain that the people they're lunging at would. If you hear joggers, skaters, or any other fast-moving people approaching from the front or behind, step out of the way, and ask your dog to sit. I try to focus my dogs' attention on a treat, which usually takes care of any urge to go after the person.

Don't Let Your Dog Roam Free

To me, this is a given. Letting a dog wander around outdoors alone is no different from letting a toddler out the door and urging her to go visit the neighbors. I realize some people let their dogs roam because it's an effortless way to let them get some exercise. But it's a mistake, for any number of reasons. First of all, your dog might be hit by a car or be hurt by another animal. Second, your dog will doubtless use your neighbors' yards or property as a toilet. Third, your dog might eat something toxic. Fourth, he might be stolen, or taken in by a concerned citizen who assumes he's a stray. Finally, if your dog isn't neutered (which I hope he is), he could be out creating puppies. If your female's in heat, she could be out getting pregnant.

Letting your dog run loose is not fair to him. If you don't have a fenced yard, then walk your dog on-leash. If your dog doesn't walk well on-leash, train him. Construct a dog run in your yard if necessary. Just don't let him roam free.

Leave Little Environmental Impact—Outdoors or In

In New York, there's an ongoing feud between the Parks Department and dog owners. The Parks Department maintains that dogs cause hundreds of thousands of dollars worth of damage to the city parks. I find that hard to believe—dogs use the park year-round, yet the damage seems to take place in the summer, when the fair-weather park users (like the people who barbeque and those who play soccer and other sports) are out in force.

But I concede that dogs can create damage, and, as responsible dog owners, it's up to us to minimize that damage. Don't let your dog dig holes in public places. Those holes can be dangerous—you, your dog, or someone else could step in one and be injured. When you walk your dog in your neighborhood, don't let him urinate on your neighbors' lawns. It can burn the grass. Again, clean up any poop.

> **▼ POOCH POINTER ▼**
>
> DOG ETIQUETTE
>
> - *Always clean up after your dog.*
> - *Don't let your dog accost other people or dogs.*
> - *Control your dog when in public.*
> - *Leave little impact on the environment.*
> - *Don't let your dog roam free.*

If you travel with your dog and stay in a hotel or motel that welcomes pets, be sure not to leave evidence that a dog stayed there. Bring along your dog's bed or crate to minimize shed hair. If you allow your dog in the bed, cover the bedspread with a sheet or blanket you bring from home. Bring chew toys so that your dog doesn't chew anything in the hotel room, and don't leave him alone in the room if he is prone to barking.

I dream of a paradise in which dogs are well-behaved and welcome everywhere. Actually, a central Florida planned community is being designed specifically for people with pets (it's called "Petville"). But most of us don't live in paradise. If we want to spend more time with our dogs, it's up to us to mind our manners and make sure that our canines mind theirs. Do your part to make your dog welcome, and you'll be helping to make other dogs welcome as well.

9 A Tired Dog Is a Happy Dog

"Help! My dog is driving me crazy!" Dog trainers and behaviorists often hear this plea from a frantic potential client. If your dog constantly gets herself into mischief, chews up your stuff, and bugs you to play, chances are she's underexercised. It's not a great way to live: She drives you nuts, you yell at her, it doesn't help, and everyone's unhappy.

▸ DON'T NEGLECT YOUR DOG'S EXERCISE NEEDS ◂

Fortunately, there's an easy cure for an underexercised dog: Tire him out! If your dog is sleeping (which he'll do if he's well-exercised), he can't get into trouble.

Pattie Lawler of Bann, Germany, says that exercise is essential for her young English springer spaniel, Charley. "Charley without exercise is like the Tasmanian devil let out of his cage," she says. When underexercised, he barks, digs, and "attacks" household objects (like boxes, his bed, and anything left on the floor) in an effort to get his owner's attention.

On the other hand, when Charley has had sufficient exercise, he occupies himself at home by napping, chewing a bone, or quietly playing with a toy.

Fifteen Minutes Every Day

"Every dog needs at least fifteen minutes a day of vigorous, playful exercise," says Deborah Wood. How vigorous? The equivalent of enough exercise to make you break out into a sweat. Each of your dog's muscles must be exercised.

The amount of that exercise varies for each individual dog, so pay attention to your dog's needs. It takes a lot more exercise to tire out a German wirehaired pointer than a pug, for example. "For a Pekingese, a walk to the corner and back might be that fifteen minutes of vigorous exercise," Wood points out.

What will regular exercise do for your dog? It'll keep her healthy, for one thing. Exercise is as important for your dog as it is for you—if not more so. Dee Blanco, D.V.M., a holistic vet in private practice in Santa Fe, New Mexico, says that regular exercise in a clean environment is an important preventive health measure for your dog. It'll also keep your dog's weight in check. Being overweight is a common problem in dogs—an estimated 40 to 60 percent of adult dogs in this country are overweight.

If your dog has aggressive tendencies, exercise will help let out pent-up emotions and to calm her. It will also help a nervous dog to be more serene.

In *The Tao of Bow Wow,* Wood calls regular exercise "the magic elixir." "One of the main reasons animals are turned into shelters is they are not getting enough exercise," she says. It's no coincidence that the majority of dogs you see in a shelter are young adults of large, active breeds or mixes.

Wood, who owns tiny papillons, knows firsthand that toy dogs need exercise, too. "People treat toy dogs like stuffed animals," she says. Fortunately, it is fairly easy to give small dogs the exercise they need. You can play a rousing game of fetch with a little dog in your own living room, while you sit in your easy chair and toss a toy.

▼ POOCH POINTER ▼

The benefits of exercise are:

- *good health (for you and your dog)*
- *weight control*
- *fewer behavioral problems*
- *outlet for pent-up emotions*
- *mental stimulation*
- *fun (for you and your dog)*

Pet-care columnist Gina Spadafori advises dog owners to take a holistic approach to behavioral problems. If your dog is exhibiting problem behavior—like excessive barking, chewing, or digging—don't look for a quick fix to the particular problem (an anti-bark collar, for instance). Instead, look for the source of the problem. Chances are that source is a lack of exercise.

"When people come to me looking for solutions to their dog's problem behavior, I always tell them to increase the dog's aerobic exercise and increase the obedience training so that both mind and body are exercised," Spadafori says.

Only after that can you start working on limiting the problem behavior.

Safety First

If your dog's been a couch potato for a while and has perhaps put on weight, don't launch into a major exercise program for her all at once. Ease her into it. You wouldn't roll off the couch, put on your sweats, and run a marathon, right? Pay attention to your dog, and slow down if she gets tired. You might need to start out walking and work your way up to jogging, for example.

What about biking? Be careful! While riding with your dog can provide some great exercise, if you're on a bike and ask your dog to jog next to you, it's easy for her to tire without your noticing. Make sure your dog is in excellent condition before you start taking her on bike rides.

If you want to bike with your dog, train her to trot next to you. You can leash her to a special bicycle attachment made for that purpose. If you're simply holding the leash in your hand, you're asking for a crash. Envision yourself biking along and your dog catching sight of a squirrel or another dog. You can't control her easily when you're on a bike. So your choice is to let go of the leash if your dog gives chase (which is dangerous for your dog), or to hold tight and lose control of your bike. Neither is an attractive option. Through proper equipment (a bike-leash attachment) and good training, you can avoid these problems.

Don't forget that your dog needs water if he's exercising. This is true no matter the season, but it's vital in the summer. I have a great little collapsible nylon water bowl that folds into its own pouch, which attaches to my belt loop. (I got it from Doggone Good, at www.doggone.com.) I carry a small bottle of water, unless I'm going somewhere where there are drinking fountains.

During the summer, use some sense, and don't exercise your dog during the heat of the day. Remember, he's wearing a fur coat and walking barefoot on the hot asphalt. Exercise is important but not when it's dangerously hot (or for that matter, dangerously cold). On hot days, try to exercise in the evenings or early mornings, whenever it's cooler.

Mental Gymnastics

Mental exercise is important for dogs, too. Getting a long run every day is great, but you should challenge your dog's mind as well. You can play hide and seek with her, teach her tricks, or play games as simple as putting a treat in one hand, holding out your closed fists, and having your dog indicate which hand holds the treat. (Then give it to her!)

Take your dog with you when you go places. Be careful not to leave her in a hot car (see chapter 15), but if it's safe for her to come along, by all means, bring her. Letting your dog go places and do things is a great way to provide mental exercise.

"Physical exercise is only half the equation," says Wood. "Mental exercise is the other half." Wood trains her dogs in competitive obedience. Other fun sports that occupy the mind as well as the body include tracking (where dogs, using only their noses, follow trails); agility (in which dogs go through an obstacle course); flyball (a relay race in which dogs run a straight course over jumps to reach a special box that releases a tennis ball when they touch it, then they race back over the jumps so the next dog can have his turn); and freestyle (in which dog-and-handler teams perform choreographed routines set to music). There are lots of other activities and sports. Check out www.dog-play.com for an exhaustive list.

Look for training facilities or clubs where you can take classes in your area. There, you and your dog can learn—gradually and safely—how to take part in these sports.

Backyard Fun

If you have a big backyard, you may not feel that you need to supply your dog with extra exercise. But that's not the case. Dogs need the stimulation of interaction with you, and they like to explore their territory. Dogs love to go on regular walks and sniff lampposts to see who's been there before them. I think of it as reading the newspaper (or checking "pee mail"). And I believe it's a vital part of Kramer and Scout's day. It goes without saying (but I'll say it anyway) that when you're exercising your dog outside of your own property, you should clean up after him.

That's not to say you shouldn't use your backyard to have fun with your dog. A good old-fashioned game of fetch can wear out your dog while you relax on the deck. Several new commercial devices allow you to throw a ball farther, with less effort. With some of them, you don't even have to pick up the slime-covered ball; the device does it for you. Look for the Go-Frrr ball; the Cool Kong, which is firmly attached to an 18-inch rope for easy throwing (and it floats!); and the Slinger, a tennis-ball slingshot. As of this writing, all were available at SitStay.com, or check a discount pet-supplies catalog.

Remember, if you don't provide an outlet for your dog's energy, she'll find one of her own. That might mean she chews the leg of your antique table, shreds books, or plays tug-of-war with your shoelaces—while you're wearing the shoes.

We ask a lot of our dogs when we leave them alone all day. Sure, many (including mine) sleep most of the day. But we owe it to them to make that slumber the deserved sleep of the weary, not just something to do to pass the time. Daily outings are, for many dogs, the highlight of their day. Do your dog a favor—concentrate on stretching her muscles and strengthening her mind.

10 All the Right Stuff

Visit any pet-supply superstore and you'll see a dazzling array of options. There are as many types of equipment for dogs as there are breeds. New products are being invented every day. All dog owners need to buy certain categories of equipment: collars, leashes, food and water bowls, grooming equipment, toys, and beds. And there's plenty of nonbasic stuff available, including products to help you when you're traveling with your dog, doggie backpacks, training devices, bags to hold treats, and pouches to hold poop bags.

When it comes to equipment, one size doesn't fit all. What you use varies according to your dog and your own comfort. The equipment left over from your last dog may or may not be appropriate for your current dog. Here's a rundown of some of the equipment options available. If you try something that doesn't seem right for your dog, don't hesitate to replace it with an item that might be more appropriate. Frequently, a trainer can help you to decide on the best equipment for your particular dog.

▸ DON'T USE EQUIPMENT THAT'S INAPPROPRIATE FOR YOUR DOG ◂

To ensure that I wasn't skewed by my personal preferences for what works for my dogs, I conducted a short survey among a group of owners with a wide variety of dogs about the equipment they use (and the equipment they no longer use). I received three dozen responses, all from experienced folks. The responses helped to influence what I've included in this guide.

Basics: Equipment Every Dog Needs

Collars and Harnesses

Every dog needs to be identified, and the most visible form of identification are collar tags. When your dog's outside, he should wear a collar with ID tags attached (or with ID information sewn or riveted onto the collar). You may, as I do, choose to attach your leash to that collar. We use a flat, nylon collar, with a quick-snap latch (like the type used on fanny packs), which I find more convenient than a buckle. I've never had a problem with these latches breaking, but strong, energetic dogs have been known to break them. A rolled leather collar is nice as well, since it has soft edges.

Ideally, for safety's sake, the collar with tags should be one that is flat so it won't choke your dog. However, if your dog's head is smaller than his neck, he may back out of his collar. A collar does you no good if it doesn't stay on your dog. For dogs like that, a martingale-type collar is the answer. The martingale has a ring on each end, with a loop of material that connects the two rings. The ring for the leash is attached to that loop. If the martingale fits your dog properly, it won't come off, because pulling on the leash tightens the collar slightly. This makes it difficult for dogs to slip out of it. They provide a certain amount of correction when tugged.

Some people find that their dogs pull when wearing a flat collar, so they like to attach the leash to a collar or harness that provides a correction to the dog for pulling. (If you train your dog not to pull, a flat collar is sufficient.) The head halter (sold under the brand names Gentle Leader, Halti, and Snoot Loop) is becoming increasingly popular as a humane piece of training equipment. The head halter has a strap that fits over the dog's nose and another that attaches behind his ears. The leash attaches to a ring under the dog's chin. The premise is that where the head goes, the body follows; the head harness allows you to lead your dog's head. The halter also provides gentle pressure that may simulate the mother dog's correction (on the back of the neck and the snout).

Susan Beisecker of Hanover, Maryland, uses a Halti to walk her 150-pound Great Dane, Venus. "The Halti is a magic instrument," she says. "Venus is a different dog with it on, and it is humane."

Pat Miller points out in an article in the June 2000 issue of *The Whole Dog Journal* that the head halter is not always magic for all dogs. "The head halter is the perfect tool for the right applications, but it is not the easy answer to every dog's leash-walking needs," she writes.

Miller says that some dogs simply can't get used to the halter. She and other dog trainers also worry about potential damage to the spine if the halter is misused. Used properly, it's not an issue. ". . . [B]ut if the owner jerks on the head halter or allows the dog to hit the end of the leash at full charge, the halter can snap the dog's head sideways, risking damage to the spine," she writes. If you're interested in a head harness as a more humane alternative to the choke collar, be sure it is fitted properly, and pair it with positive reinforcement for not pulling. *Never* jerk on it.

Prong collars are medieval-looking devices with blunt-edged prongs all the way around. When the leash is pulled tight, the prongs apply uncomfortable pressure to the dog's neck, which usually stops the dog from pulling. Many dog trainers recommend the prong collar as an alternative to the traditional choke chain. Penny Bolton uses a prong collar for her Brittany/English springer spaniel mix, Daisy Mae, who is a confirmed puller. "The prong stops her from pulling and allows us to both enjoy the walk," she says.

▼ POOCH POINTER ▼

EQUIPMENT BASICS AND EXTRAS

Essential equipment you need for your dog:

- ***collar***
- ***leash***
- ***tags***
- ***food and water bowls***
- ***grooming equipment***
- ***toys***
- ***bed***
- ***crate***
- ***ex-pen***

Optional extras you and your dog might enjoy:

- ***sweater or coat***
- ***booties***
- ***paw wax to protect from ice and snow***
- ***collapsible crate for travel***
- ***backpack***
- ***portable water bowl***
- ***poop bag holder***
- ***interactive toys***

Choke chains, or training collars, as their proponents call them, were once a staple in homes with dogs. When pulled, this collar of choice for the traditional jerk-and-praise training method tightens around the dog's neck. The choke chain isn't harmful if used properly—the handler applies a quick-jerk correction to the collar. Unfortunately, it's rarely used properly. A pulling dog apparently gets used to the choking sensation, since he will just pull and pull while making choking sounds. Bolton's dog, Daisy Mae, used to pull on her choke collar until she vomited. With the prong collar, she doesn't pull.

Another option for pulling dogs is the traditional body harness, which won't stop your dog from pulling (sled dogs use harnesses, after all), but it won't *hurt* your pulling dog. A harness is particularly appropriate for dogs that have damaged their trachea by pulling with a collar. That's why Linda Weiss uses a body harness on her cocker spaniel, Barney, whom she adopted when he was five. Barney always wears a collar with an ID tag, but Weiss hooks Barney's leash to the harness. "We don't use a leash on his collar because he has a weakened trachea from his first five years with his other humans, who kept him on a chain. He apparently hit the end of the chain many times. The harness doesn't put any pressure on his neck."

Leashes

Leashes come in a variety of sizes and colors, but the most commonly used can be boiled down to two types: (1) the 6-foot-and-shorter traditional leash; and (2) the retractable leash.

For city walking, most dogs are tethered to a leather or nylon leash 6 feet or less in length. They're great for maintaining control of your dog. Leather is easier on the hands than nylon, though nylon is less expensive. Nylon also has the advantage of being colorful: you can have collar-and-leash "outfits" for your dog, if you so desire. Holly Kruse of Lexington, Kentucky, prefers a leather lead for walking her Irish setters. "I love a soft, weathered leather leash," she says. "Nylon leashes are too slippery and too hard on my hands when I'm walking three rambunctious setters together for a couple of miles in the city."

The downside to the 6-foot leash is that your dog can't get much exercise on it. In an ideal world, you'll use the 6-foot leash to walk your dog to an area where it is safe for him to run around off-leash.

The retractable leash (the most popular brand of retractable leash is the German-made Flexi) is the leash of choice for those who want their dogs to be able to get a lot of on-leash exercise. Retractable leashes, for the most part, are actually cords rather than straps. The first 15 inches or so of a Flexi leash (the end nearest the collar) are made of a wider strap, but the rest of the leash is a cord. Constant tension on that cord allows it to wind around itself, like a fishing line, inside the leash's bulky plastic handle. If you don't touch the thumb brake on the handle, your dog can walk any distance from you—to the end of the leash—without any slack leash getting in the way. Flexi leashes come in 16- and 26-foot lengths.

I use a retractable leash with Kramer and Scout. If I'd brought them up in New York, I probably wouldn't have gone with this type, but we moved here after both had become accustomed to them in St. Louis, where all their exercise was on-leash. Retractable leads seem to garner strong opinions: You either love them or you hate them.

I can see the flaws in the retractable leash: They apply constant pressure to the dog's neck and can encourage pulling. Kramer's almost always at the end of the leash, but he's not pulling. Scout usually lags behind, sniffing, so the tension doesn't seem to affect her. The cord is dangerous if you get it wrapped around your legs. I've had my bare legs ripped to shreds by it. The handle is bulky, and it can be challenging to hold two in one hand.

But the freedom retractable leashes allow the dog is great. It's hard to go back to a shorter lead. Plus, not having to deal with stepping around slack lead is also convenient.

Bowls

I used to use plastic bowls for my dogs' food and water. Then I read in *The Whole Dog Journal* that plastic bowls can contain cancer-causing substances, like formaldehyde, chlorine, and certain resins. That's particularly problematic if you heat the bowl or add hot water to the food. Ceramic bowls are fine, as long as the glaze is nontoxic. Your safest bet is to buy ceramic bowls that are made in the United States. Stainless-steel bowls are also a good choice, because bacteria doesn't accumulate in them. They clean easily, and you can pop them into the dishwasher.

Grooming Equipment

The grooming equipment you'll need depends upon your dog's coat. (See chapter 18 for more information on the importance of grooming.) But at the bare minimum, you'll need a brush of some sort, toenail clippers, and shampoo. Chances are you'll need a lot more than that! Check with your breeder or a professional groomer to find out about the right grooming equipment for your type of dog—and how to use it.

Crates and Ex-Pens

A crate is a great thing. Nearly every one of the respondents to my survey uses and endorses them. (See chapter 11 for more information on crating your dog.) Whether you get a plastic Vari-Kennel-type crate or a wire one depends upon your dog and your own sensibilities. Whichever you get, make sure it's high quality, since you'll be using it for many years. This is particularly important if you're planning to fly your dog in his crate (in which case, you'll have to use a plastic crate). It's essential that a crate that's flown can withstand lots of handling.

Ex-pens (short for exercise pens) are 4-foot-high, 2-foot-wide panels of wire fencing that attach to one another. Ex-pens can be used to create a long-term confinement area when you're housetraining a dog or before he's given freedom of the house. They also make a swell puppy playpen for when you're home with your puppy. "Ex-pens are great," says Andrea Arden. "I don't think enough people know about them." (See chapter 2 for more information on using ex-pens with puppies.)

Ex-pens are particularly helpful for people with multiple dogs. You can take more than one dog to a class or the park to train. Use an ex-pen as a holding area for the other dogs, while you work with a particular dog. "I don't know how I lived without my ex-pen!" says Ann Daugherty of Reno, Nevada. "I use an ex-pen at home, when I need to separate my dogs for some reason. I take one to the park to practice obedience: one dog out working, the other waiting in the ex-pen in the shade."

This chapter covers the absolute basics. Your dog will also need toys and a bed—and she'll doubtless help you decide about those items. Just be careful when introducing a new toy or bed. Watch your dog with it to make sure she doesn't tear it up, trying to consume small pieces that could choke her or create an obstruction.

If you're like me, you'll start collecting dog stuff just for the fun of it. By the time your dog's a senior citizen, you'll have an amazing collection. The Resources section lists some discount catalogs for bargains and specialty Web sites where you can find unusual items.

11 Give Him a Den to Call His Own

Though it may look like a cage to you, a crate—either the wire or plastic type airlines use to ship dogs—can be a cozy haven for your dog. A crate has a multitude of uses: It's instrumental in housetraining, it keeps a young dog out of harm's way, and it's a place where your dog can go to get away from it all. Dogs—like their wolf and fox cousins—are, after all, den animals.

But a crate can also be misused. Leaving a dog in a crate so long that she soils in it is cruel, since a dog's natural instinct is to not soil where she sleeps. Using time in the crate as punishment is unwise—you jeopardize your dog's pleasant associations with the crate. You want your dog to see it as the happy, safe place it can be.

DON'T MISTAKE CONFINEMENT FOR IMPRISONMENT

"People totally misunderstand confinement," says Ian Dunbar. "They look on confinement as a prison, and they just don't understand how you use a crate, for example, to housetrain a dog." Used properly, a crate can be a key part of housetraining. Dunbar's housetraining method, which uses a crate as well as a long-term confinement area (like a bathroom), is discussed in chapter 2.

When we first brought Kramer home as a puppy, I didn't like the idea of a crate. I searched high and low for a book that didn't advocate crating. It took a while, but I found one. (I should have been less bullheaded and considered why the majority of dog-care books advised using crates.)

In the first week with our new puppy, we made little progress with house-training—and we had a little monster on our hands. We had to watch him constantly, except when he was asleep. We kept him in a bathroom when we weren't home and, of course, he urinated on the floor. Just as important, we had nowhere to put him when he would go through the puppy crazies and needed a time-out.

At the end of that exasperating week, we borrowed a crate. It made a world of difference. We confined Kramer in the crate for short periods during the day, and promptly took him outside when he got out. We were well on our way to having a housetrained puppy by the time we went back to work, three weeks after he joined our family. And I worked close enough from home to be able to stop in during the day to let him out.

Andrea Arden likens a crate to a playpen used for children. "It is exactly the same concept as a playpen or crib. The only difference is a lid on the crate," she says.

Introducing the Crate

Some dogs take to crates like a fish to water. Others don't. In our household, Kramer's always been fine in his crate. Scout, who came to us when she was three, just hates it. Even if your dog doesn't seem to care for being in a crate, it's to your advantage to put in the effort to get her used to it. I wish I had: I wouldn't have to worry about leaving Scout at the vet or the groomer, and I could take both dogs to training class and crate the one who's not being worked.

It's up to you to make the crate a pleasant place for your dog. Give her something to do in there, like chewing on a hollow rubber toy stuffed with food and treats. Putting your dog in her crate should be the doggie equivalent of parking a child in front of Nintendo.

If your dog puts up a fuss about being in a crate, it's a good idea to feed her inside of it. Ian Dunbar recommends breaking up the meals and serving several a day. Start by tossing a few pieces of kibble into the crate. Your dog will probably go in to get it, and then come right out again. After three or four sessions like this, toss in some kibble, then shut the door when she goes in. Immediately feed her some more kibble through the bars. Let her out, and ignore her for a few minutes. Try it again, and then ignore her for a little longer. Next time, put your dog in the crate with a stuffed Kong. What you've accomplished is teaching your dog that she gets attention, toys, and food when she's in the crate. That should help to make the association pleasant.

Some dogs are fine in their crates while they're eating but put up a fuss when they've finished. Others just don't like being alone. Ann Daugherty, who has several Samoyeds, taught her puppy Gracie not to fuss this way: She put Gracie in her crate, then sat on the bed next to the crate. When Gracie was quiet, Daugherty reached for the door. As soon as the puppy barked, whined, or jumped at the door, Daugherty pulled her hand away and moved farther from the crate. She'd leave the room with Gracie in the crate (over her protestations), and reenter when the dog was quiet. As soon as Gracie started to bark, Daugherty left the room again. "Gradually, she was quiet longer, and I could walk across the room to open her door," recalls Daugherty. "It took her a while to get it, but she did figure it out, and now will firmly plant her little white butt and quietly wait for me."

The Crate in Housetraining

The main benefit of using a crate in housetraining is that as den animals, dogs instinctively don't like to soil where they sleep. So if you crate them, they'll hold it as long as they can. It's up to you to make sure you're not asking them to hold it too long. Dunbar says that an eight-week-old puppy has the capacity to hold his urine for only seventy-five minutes. That's why the long-term confinement area is so important.

When you let your dog out of the crate, she'll almost certainly need to pee. Here's your opportunity to hustle her outside and have her pee in the appropriate area. Then you can give her treats. She learns quickly that delicious treats appear when she pees outside.

Kelly Graham of Mayfield, Ohio, who has nine greyhounds and a whippet, is a proponent of crate training. She crates certain dogs when she's not home, as well as feeds her dogs in their crates. "Crates keep dogs safe," she says. Not only do they keep dogs safe from one another and from household hazards, but they also keep the household safe from dogs, Graham points out.

▼ POOCH POINTER ▼

CRATE DOS AND DON'TS

Do keep the crate in your bedroom. Dogs like to sleep with their human pack members. If you isolate your dog in another room, she may cry out of loneliness.

Do have a household rule that your dog is not to be disturbed in his crate. This provides him with a precious, safe haven from household stresses, particularly kids and visitors.

Do teach your dog to be comfortable in her crate when you are at home. Ginny Debbink of Long Valley, New Jersey, wishes she'd done this. "My dogs will willingly go into their crates, but they're deeply insulted if they are expected to stay there once they realize I'm still in the house," she says. This becomes an issue when you have to let workers who aren't dog-friendly come into the house. Give your dog time in the crate (with suitable recreation) while you're at home.

Don't use the crate as punishment. It should be a happy place for your dog, so don't toss him in there if he misbehaves.

Don't leave your dog in the crate too long. If you plan to be away for more than a couple of hours (or more than an hour, if you have a tiny puppy), use the long-term confinement area. You ruin the crate as a housetraining device if you force your dog to eliminate in it. (See chapter 2 for more information.)

Don't reinforce your dog's negative behavior in the crate. Ignore her if she's complaining. The worst thing you can do is to tolerate whining and crying, and then finally give in by paying her some attention. If you do that, you've taught her that if she carries on long enough, she'll eventually get your attention.

Traveling

If your dog is accustomed to a crate, you can take her wherever *you* go. If you stay with your dog in a motel and you leave her for short periods of time, you can leave her in her crate without worrying about a hotel worker accidentally letting her loose.

If your car can accommodate a crate, your dog will travel more safely than if she is loose. Be sure to tie down the crate so that in the event of an accident it doesn't become a heavy missile.

If you take your dog somewhere that requires air travel and your dog is too large to fit in a bag under the seat in front of you, she will have to travel in an airline-approved crate in the cargo hold. As nerve-racking as that surely is for both dog and owner, it must be easier on a dog who is accustomed to spending time in a crate.

Feeding

In multidog households, crates can be a great way to separate your dogs while they eat. Feeding dogs too near one another can be asking for trouble. Even if your dogs get along famously, fights can erupt pretty quickly over a dropped morsel. Feeding them separately also prevents one dog from stealing another's food. Crates are an easy way to separate your dogs at feeding time. Doing so also fosters a positive association with the crate.

Illness and Injury

If your dog needs to spend time at the vet's office without you, it will be easier on her if she's crate-trained. A pet hospital will appreciate a properly crate-trained dog when that dog has to spend several days there.

Once your dog is home, she might require crate rest. That was the case with Scout when she joined our family. She came to us with a broken leg, and for safety's sake, and to keep her from getting boisterous with Kramer, we crated her when we weren't at home. She never grew to love the crate (and I wasn't as savvy about ways to get her to enjoy it). My life (and hers) would have been much more pleasant if I'd taken the time to crate-train her.

Wire or Plastic?

Choosing a plastic airline crate (typically known as a Vari-Kennel for its most prominent manufacturer) or a wire crate is a matter of personal preference. The Vari-Kennel is more denlike, while wire allows your dog to be more aware of his surroundings—which can be good or bad, depending on your dog.

Wire crates have the advantage of being roomier. Unlike the plastic crates, their interior dimensions are very close to the exterior dimensions. The Vari-Kennel, for example, has a deep lip on the front and a smaller lip around its perimeter, which subtracts inches from the interior.

However, plastic crates are much lighter and therefore easier to clean. They're also quieter (though by no means silent) when the dog moves around inside.

That crate we were so reluctant to use when Kramer was a puppy has turned into one of his favorite places. We chose the plastic kind, and we've had to remove the door for lack of space. On his own, Kramer goes into his crate to sleep at least once a day. It may not be the most attractive piece of furniture we own (though it does provides a nice surface for storing stuff), but it's one of the most important.

12 Be the Leader

The concept of total equality is a human ideal. People aspire to relationships in which both parties are treated equally, but dogs just aren't like that. Their ancestors, wolves, lived in packs, and within the pack is a strict hierarchy. There's the big kahuna, the leader, and below him, each member of the pack has a position. When there's dissension, it's frequently a struggle over rank. You and your family are your dog's pack. You don't want that kind of struggle occurring in your home.

▸ DON'T SET UP POWER STRUGGLES ◂

Your dog expects there to be a leader of the pack. Many dogs are perfectly happy to be led, but if there isn't a clear leader, they may feel the need to pick up the slack. "Dogs need a leader in order to be comfortable," says Myrna Milani, D.V.M., and author of *DogSmart,* who has a private consulting practice that deals with bond/behavior issues. "If the owner doesn't communicate that he is in charge, the dog has no choice but to assume leadership."

Being your dog's leader doesn't mean you have to buy into the old-fashioned practice of the alpha roll, where you're advised to physically turn your dog over onto his back and pin him there to prove you're the boss. You can be a leader without being forceful, says dog trainer Pat Miller. "I believe in a policy of benevolent leadership, as opposed to intimidating or dictatorial leadership," she says.

Miller points out that the old model of physical domination over your dog, which was purportedly based on how wolves interact, is faulty on two counts. First, a pack's true alpha dog does not throw his weight around. He is respected and therefore goes unchallenged by the other dogs. "A good canine pack leader doesn't run around roughing up his packmates," says Miller.

The second misconception about alpha dogs is that they put other dogs down on their backs (which is what the alpha roll is supposed to simulate). In reality, a dog who feels intimidated by another dog willingly rolls on his back to show submission. The intimidator doesn't physically force him into that position.

So the role of the benevolent dictator is, in fact, the one that mimics wild canines. If you're the benevolent dictator over your dog—that is, you control his behavior and not the other way around—both of you will be happier.

Establishing Hierarchy Through Leadership Exercises

Establishing leadership with your dog is not difficult. By performing some simple exercises every day, you can remind your dog that you're the pack leader.

The basic idea behind being your dog's leader is that she should look to you for what she needs, and she should earn what you give her. Basic tenets of the program include no free feeding (she should be fed at times you determine), and no free treats. Ask her to sit, or do something else before you reward her.

One of Miller's favorite leadership tricks is the "wait-at-the-door" exercise. The doorway provides a useful tool for working with your dog, because he goes in and out of the door so often each day. This offers the opportunity to remind your dog to do what you ask, Miller says.

Before you open the door to let your dog outside, have her sit and wait. Or, if you prefer, have her lie down and wait. Open the door, then release your dog. Miller has four dogs, so she'll frequently release them one at a time, in varying order. What does she do if one of her dogs exits the door without waiting? "I invite her back in and have her wait again, and then she's the last one to go out," she says. She doesn't yell, and she doesn't grab or physically restrain her dog.

Miller frequently uses food rewards in training, but with the wait-at-the-door exercise, she says, a food reward isn't necessary. Being allowed to run out the door is the reward—it's what Miller calls a "life reward."

Your dog doesn't have to wait for you to go through the door first; he just needs to wait for you to tell him it's okay. "For a long time, there's been a myth that leaders always go through the door first," says Miller. "I don't believe that." By waiting at an open door for permission, your dog gets the message that you're the leader.

Another exercise is calling your dog frequently when he's out in the yard. If your dog's off playing, call him, and then reward him with a food treat when he comes to you. This constantly reminds him that coming back to you when you ask him to is a good thing, Miller says.

I use this recall practice frequently with my dogs when we're at the off-leash park. I always have treats at the ready, and my dogs come reliably—with joy on their faces. It's one of the most rewarding things I've done in training them.

A Lack of Leadership Can Result in Aggression

The majority of Milani's consulting practice as a veterinary ethologist involves aggressive dogs. In most cases, the aggression results from the relationship between owner and dog. "Hands down, across the board, the biggest mistake owners make is that they, knowingly or unknowingly, relate to their dogs as littermates rather than as a good bitch to a pup," she says. If you act like a good bitch—that is, like a benevolent leader—the question of who is in charge does not come up and there is no reason for a power struggle.

If, at the outset of your relationship with your dog, you establish yourself as the benevolent dictator, then you will likely preempt a host of potential behavioral problems. If you're already having some problems with your dog, then starting some of these exercises now may help.

Being a dog's leader is more effortless for some people/dog pairs than for others. You might naturally fall into a relationship with your dog in which you are the leader. But if you're not a born leader and your dog has ambitions for leadership, you may be in for some problems. "Depending on the dog, leadership sometimes needs to be a more focused effort," Miller says.

If your dog wants to be the leader, he tends to be in greater control of the relationship than is healthy, she says. But even if your dog doesn't really want to be the leader, it can be problematic if you abdicate your leadership role. "Sometimes it just causes confusion in the relationship rather than does real, serious harm,"

Miller says. "The dog tends not to be under control but isn't doing things that are dangerous."

However, in the absence of your leadership, there's always the chance that even a timid dog will decide that his job is to protect you—which could become dangerous to other people. All he really needs is your reassurance that you're in charge of allowing people into the house.

Dogs who really want to be the leader (some people call these dogs "dominant") can indeed be dangerous if they're allowed to take over. If you're experiencing severe behavioral problems with your dog, particularly if he is acting aggressively, or you feel in any way threatened by him, seek professional help. An animal behaviorist or a highly skilled dog trainer should be able to assist you.

A dog's behavior is a reflection of the relationship between the dog and the owner, says Milani. "Trying to change the behavior without changing the relationship is like trying to change the mirror because you don't like what you see in it," she says.

Finding Help

If you feel you must hire a behaviorist or trainer—a smart move if your dog is trying to take over as leader—find one whose methods you are comfortable with. Trust your instincts: If the expert asks you to do something to your dog that doesn't feel right, look elsewhere.

If your dog seeks a higher rank than you, then using old-fashioned, force-based leadership methods could truly backfire. For example, you might be bitten if you try to force a dog into an alpha roll. If your dog bites you, many of the experts who recommended the alpha roll in the first place would now recommend that you euthanize your aggressive dog.

Miller recalls a client's dog, a five-month-old English setter, that perfectly illustrates the contrast between benevolent leadership and force-based leadership. This young dog is a real gentleman, says Miller. But as a confident, self-contained dog, he objected to the force-based methods that his owner was trying to use in order to get him to behave at the groomer's and the veterinary hospital. On the advice of the groomer, vet, and breeder, the owner was physically placing and holding the dog down on the grooming table in a battle of wills. The animal-care professionals told her that she must physically fight it out with her dog—and that she had to win.

The client was considering euthanizing the young setter because people were telling her that he would become dangerous. Miller agreed that if she had continued to use the force-based methods, there was a good chance the dog would indeed bite this owner.

But Miller demonstrated that the forceful methods weren't necessary. She began working with the dog, using a clicker (a small box that makes a sharp click when pressed). Here, the trainer rewards behavior by first identifying it with a click, then following up the click with a reward (usually a food treat). Soon, the dog begins to offer behaviors in order to get a click.

This dog took to clicker training like a fish to water, as did his owner. In about an hour's time, the dog was willingly jumping onto (and staying on) the grooming table. He was under control. Miller sent the client home with some leadership exercises and instructions on clicker training, and is confident the two will have a great relationship.

Another reason to be wary of force-based training or leadership techniques, is that some dogs are branded dominant when their aggression actually stems from fear and self-protection. It's important not to use harsh methods with these dogs, since such practices will only make a fearful dog more frightened. That's why it's so important to follow your gut and to seek professionals who use positive, humane training methods.

The Importance of Training and Leadership

Training is a critical part of establishing leadership with your dog, Miller says. To let your dog know that you're his leader, you must open the lines of communication. If your dog pays you no mind, you're certainly not leading him. A great way to "communicate" with your dog is through continuous training. (See chapter 12 for more about training.) "If you and your dog know how to communicate with each other, there is a greater level of respect on both sides," says Miller.

Training doesn't take place in the classroom alone.

"Every time you interact with your dog, it's a training opportunity," she says. "And a training opportunity is a leadership opportunity."

When you interact with your dog on a walk, you're training him. You may not be asking him to do specific things, and you may not even be offering food rewards, or clicking your clicker when you get the desired behavior, but you're letting him know what behaviors you like. You're training him for real life.

Because many dog owners are forced to spend so much time away from their dog, their relationship is plagued by guilt, says Milani. Like absentee parents who have custody of their children only on weekends, the dog owner doesn't want the time he does get to spend with his dog to be full of training, limit setting, or leadership exercises. Many people want to be a best friend to their dog rather than a parent. This doesn't work any better in human-dog relationships than it does in parent-child relationships. Be your dog's leader. He'll thank you for it.

13 Reinforce Good Behavior

Dog training. For some people, the phrase conjures up images of dogs and people repetitively practicing boring exercises. Some folks think dog-training classes teach dogs a bunch of skills they'll never need in real life. Others think obedience classes are only for those who want to compete with their dogs in the obedience ring.

Training has evolved in recent years. If you find the right trainer, who uses the more modern methods, you'll be using positive reinforcement, food, and other rewards to get your dog to choose to do what you want rather than using force to get him to yield to your wishes. And not only is dog training fun nowadays, it is absolutely essential if you want your dog—large or small—to be a valued member of your family.

▸ DON'T UNDERESTIMATE THE VALUE OF TRAINING ◂

"I think that dog training has a bad image," says Andrea Arden. "Part of the reason people avoid training is that they think, with training, the dog becomes a robot and has no will of his own. That's not the truth. Training is actually fun."

Training can turn a canine terrorist into a well-mannered dog. It gives you the tools—the common language—to help shape your dog's behavior. Training won't change your dog's personality. But if he's naturally a mischief maker, it might help you to channel that energy a little more productively.

What Good Dogs Should Know

As we discussed in chapter 4, dogs are dogs. On a daily basis we ask them to go against their hardwired instincts in order to fit into our society. It's important not to deny your dog her doggie nature. So the next time your dog does something that inconveniences you or makes you mad (for instance, rolling in something stinky), remind yourself that she's a dog and what she's doing is natural.

You can, however, help to avoid certain problems by teaching your dog basic manners and doing what trainers call "training an incompatible behavior." The more things she'll do when you ask her, the more opportunities you have to keep her out of trouble. The six basic skills every dog should learn are:

- sit
- look at me
- come when called
- down
- stay
- walk nicely on a leash

"Sit"

"Sit" will help you to manage your dog in almost any situation. For example, if your dog greets your guests by jumping on them, you can ask her to do something she can't possibly do while jumping up, like sitting. Don't let your guests give her any attention (positive or negative) until she sits. If her excitement level is too high and she just can't contain herself long enough to sit, you can help her by attaching a leash to her collar or head halter; ask her to sit before you answer the door, and then stand on the leash to keep your dog from breaking her sit.

"Look at Me"

How can this command possibly keep a dog out of trouble? If you train your dog to look at your face when you request it (by saying "look at me," "cookie," the dog's name, or whatever word or phrase suits you), you can divert her attention from things—like other dogs—that might cause her to misbehave.

"Look at me" also teaches your dog to pay attention to you. At any moment, you might say out of the blue, "look at me" and all your dog has to do is to comply to get a treat. This provides great motivation for your dog to perk up her ears when you speak to her.

"It all begins with attention," Arden says, "because if you don't have a dog that gives you any consideration, you can't train any of the other stuff anyway."

Your attention word should be something other than your dog's name, she advises. "People tend to wear out the dog's name." I know I say my dogs' names all the time. I wouldn't want to have to reward them each time.

The key to this attention game is to associate good things with your attention word or phrase. Say "look at me," or another word or phrase (Arden uses "treat"), and when your dog complies, give her a treat, or a ball, or take her for a walk. "Always associate that word with something good," Arden says.

"Come"

Coming when called (which trainers term a *recall*) is an important skill all dogs should learn to perform reliably. If you plan to let your dog off-leash, this skill is imperative.

I'm not a dog trainer, so I won't attempt to show you how to train your dog in this book. I list some excellent training books in the Recommended Reading section. I'll limit myself to making some observations about training mistakes I see people make.

Each day, Kramer, Scout, and I go to Prospect Park here in Brooklyn, where dogs are allowed off-leash during certain hours. Here, I have ample opportunity to watch people interact with their dogs.

I think the number one mistake—and I see it all the time—is made by people who call their dogs to them and then yell at them when the dog comes. A friendly white-and-brown pit bull once came running up to Kramer and Scout.

The dogs briefly interacted, and then the dog's owner started calling his dog from across the field. He didn't walk over to get his dog, mind you, but just called him angrily. The dog trotted back to his owner, and as I was admiring that recall, the owner bent over and started wagging his finger at the dog, admonishing him for having left him to greet my dogs. The pit bull cowered, then slunk past his owner.

Not ten minutes later, the dog was back visiting us, and the routine was repeated. The owner gave him the same (obviously ineffective) scolding.

Rather than shout at his dog, I think the man should have praised his dog to high heaven for coming when called. I'm blessed that my dogs don't wander too far from me; but thanks to the treats I keep in my pocket, my dogs come running when I call! They're always rewarded, never yelled at!

If your dog wanders away from you, and you feel you need to admonish him, it's a better idea to go to him, tell him "no" if you absolutely must, and then clip on his leash and take him away from the forbidden area. Why in the world would your dog want to leave somewhere fun to come to you if he knows when he gets there that he will be in trouble?

"Down" and "Stay"

A solid recall can be a lifesaver, since it allows you to call your dog away from a dangerous situation. But that assumes it's safe for your dog to run to you.
"I see a lot of emergencies where it's actually better not to call your dog; it's better to say 'down!' " says Arden.

If you're on the other side of the street from your dog, for example, you don't want him to run into the street to come when called. If your dog will perform a down, with you at a distance, or if he'll hold a rock-solid stay, you can protect him even more. It's worth training and practicing these skills even if you don't find you need them on a daily basis.

Walking Nicely On-Leash

I'm not asking you to have your dog heel precisely at your left side all of the time, but walking him is more pleasant if he has been trained to walk nicely on a loose leash. With proper, positive training, you can teach your dog not to pull without choke chains or prong collars. If your dog is trained to walk nicely, walks become more pleasant for both of you and, consequently, you take more of them. You and your dog get more exercise, spend more time together, and your dog is exposed to more interesting things. It's a win-win situation. That's why it's such an important skill to teach your dog. Again, the books in the Recommended Reading section will show you how, as could a good, positive class.

The "New Wave" in Dog Training

"I get chills when I think about the ways dog training is changing," Arden says. If you had visited the average dog-training class only a decade ago, you would have seen dogs with choke chains around their necks walking in a large circle with their owners, and being yanked into position when they wandered from their owner's left knee. You might have seen the instructor advise an owner to grab the dog by the scruff of the neck and shake him in order to show him who's boss. You might have seen the teacher turn a dog over onto his back (the infamous alpha roll)—and you might have seen that dog scream in submission. You might even have seen the instructor grab a dog's leash out of the owner's hand, jerk the chain so that the dog's front feet were lifted off the floor, and yell at the dog. In fact, I saw every one of these things in Kramer's traditional-style obedience classes in 1992.

Fast forward to 2000. If you visit a dog-training class now—at least any class that I'd recommend you take—you're likely to see some dogs in flat collars and others wearing head halters (like a horse). You might see box-shaped clickers in the owners' hands. Using the principles of operant conditioning, the owners click when their dog performs a behavior they like. The dog gets a tasty treat after the click. (The click allows the owner to tell the dog precisely what behavior he is being rewarded for.) You might see an owner turn her back on her misbehaving dog, completely ignoring the bad behavior until it stops. You'll likely see lots of happy recalls.

Dog training is a lot more fun than it used to be, plain and simple. If you visit a class and it doesn't look fun, keep looking.

Should You Take a Class?

There are several ways to go about training your dog. You can try to do it yourself, using books like those listed in the Recommended Reading section. You can take a group class, or you can take private lessons.

I'd advise going with an expert rather than trying to do it yourself. No book can substitute for the personal attention of your instructor, though books can be great for backup.

Group or private? It depends on your dog. If your dog has specialized needs (a specific behavioral problem or a particular fear, for example) that might not be addressed in a group class, it probably makes sense to take private lessons, at least until you get the special circumstance under control.

But if you're interested in basic training, and your dog doesn't have a violent reaction to other dogs, group classes have the advantage of exposing your dog to lots of other dogs. You also make friends with the other dog owners. You can show off your dog's skills to others, and when those skills are a little lacking, you can commiserate with empathetic classmates.

What I don't recommend you do is send your dog off to be trained at another location. It sounds attractive: Your unruly pooch leaves home for a week or two and comes back a saint. I just don't see it happening. Sure, by the time he was sent home, your dog was probably obeying the person who was training him. But that might not translate to his obeying you. A big part of

▼ POOCH POINTER ▼

HOW TO FIND A TRAINER

Finding a trainer in your community can be challenging. Some ways to start your search are listed below. No matter how you locate one, observe the trainer in action before hiring her or enrolling in a class. Make sure you're comfortable with her training techniques.

- *word of mouth*
- *asking people you see with well-behaved dogs*
- *the Association of Pet Dog Trainers' Web site (www.apdt.org)*
- *the clicker teachers' listing Web site (www.wazoo.com/~marge/Clicker_Trainers/Clicker_Trainers.html)*
- *ads or articles in community dog-related newsletters and magazines*
- *dog-related community events*

taking classes with your dog is learning how to work with her. In fact, most instructors concentrate on training people to train their dogs, not training the actual canine students.

What to Look for in a Trainer

Ask to visit a class before you enroll. A reputable trainer will allow you to sit in on his class. "Always visit, no matter what," Arden advises.

When you're there, make sure you're comfortable with how the instructor interacts with the students. Observe methods, and make sure they're ones you'd be comfortable performing with your dog. I encourage you to look for the more modern methods mentioned above. They're not only more fun, they're also easier on your dog. They don't have the undesirable side effects that correction-based training can have.

Trust your instincts. If you enroll in a class that you end up being uncomfortable in, there's no shame in quitting. I dropped out of a therapy-dog class that Scout and I were enrolled in. The methods were too harsh, and I felt terrible complying with them. I hated to be a quitter, but I was flooded with feelings of relief when I withdrew from that hated class. I'm sure Scout was relieved, too.

Wendy Hudson of Minneapolis-St. Paul had a similar experience. She and her Labrador retriever, Brenna, were enrolled in a class with a big-name trainer in her area. "The trainer was militaristic, not fun," recalls Hudson. "Brenna just shut down after a while and would dribble urine from the stress." Hudson has found a more positive, informal club and plans to enroll Brenna. "Maybe I can have the dream of a CD yet." (A CD, which stands for Companion Dog, is an AKC obedience title.)

Training provides you and your dog with a common language. If you master the aforementioned six commands, the two of you should be able to enjoy a relatively trouble-free life together.

These commands can form the basis for sports and activities you can do together (like agility, herding, obedience, or therapy work, to name just a few). A trained dog is welcome in more places, so you'll spend more time with your dog. And, if you ask me, that kind of companionship is what having a dog is all about.

14 Talk—and Listen—to Your Dog

If you have any kind of relationship with your dog, you know that he is constantly communicating with you. You may not even be aware of how closely tuned in you are to his body language. You also have an emotional connection with your animal; don't you have an idea of what he is feeling, at least some of the time?

Communicating with your dog—and it's a two-way street, as communication occurs in both directions—is an important aspect of your relationship with him. If you pay attention, you can pick up important clues as to how your dog feels about you, others, and certain situations. It's up to you to open yourself up to receive that communication.

▸ DON'T MISTAKE THE ABSENCE OF LANGUAGE FOR A LACK OF COMMUNICATION ◂

Just because your dog doesn't speak to you in words doesn't mean he isn't communicating. We communicate with our dogs (and they with us) through a variety of channels. Body language is surely well known (though not always easy for the average person to interpret). Norwegian dog trainer and enthusiast Turid Rugaas's groundbreaking book, *On Talking Terms with Dogs: Calming Signals,* reveals that dogs try to avoid altercations, and communicate their peaceful intentions through a series of signals they send to one another, which Rugaas has dubbed calming signals. Once you become aware of these signals, you see dogs use them all the time, and you can use them on your dog.

I firmly believe that dogs can understand us when we speak out loud to them. The more verbal we are with them, the more attuned they are to our language. You don't have to limit yourself to one-word commands when you're communicating with your dog. Many dog owners who are emotionally connected with their dogs speak in complete sentences, and many dogs understand.

Dogs and humans also have a telepathic connection. In 1999, I wrote a book about telepathic communication with animals, called *You Can Talk to Your*

▼ POOCH POINTER ▼

HOW HUMANS AND DOGS COMMUNICATE

BODY LANGUAGE: *Dogs communicate with one another—and with us—through body language. For example, a tucked tail signals fear or submission. A stiff stance, with erect ears and tail, communicates dominance. Pay attention to your dog's body language, and you'll have a window to his feelings.*

VERBAL LANGUAGE: *Dogs who live with us understand more spoken language than you might think. Speak in full sentences to your canine; you might well see him respond to what you say.*

TELEPATHIC COMMUNICATION: *Dogs and humans communicate mind-to-mind all the time. Open your mind to the possibility that the dog-related words and feelings that pop into your head are actually coming from your dog. Try sending your dog mental images and silent words. You'll be surprised at how this practice strengthens your bond.*

Animals: Animal Communicators Tell You How. Through my research, I concluded that the telepathic connection is real, and that humans simply need to open themselves to it in order to enjoy a fuller relationship with their animals.

Body Language

Most of us are aware of the common stances dogs take to communicate with other canines. For example, dogs who stand stiffly, with ears and tail up, are communicating dominance. A crouching dog, with ears flat and tail tucked under, is communicating submission.

It's much more complicated than that, of course. While it's important (and fun) to watch your dog's body language with other dogs, it's his body language with you that will be really revealing.

As we discussed in chapter 12, hierarchy is important to dogs, and if your dog doesn't see you as his leader, he has no choice but to take on the role himself, says Myrna Milani.

Part of the confusion about who's in charge relates to body language. Your dog may be communicating his role as the leader without your really knowing it. If he jumps on you, for example, you might find that endearing. But it may be his way of displaying dominance. If your dog demands that you pet him, you may be more than happy to oblige. But in doing so, you're feeding into his leadership role. If the dog's behavior escalates into aggression—as many of Milani's cases do—you'll likely be advised to become your dog's leader and turn that body language around.

When she consults with a new client, Milani asks about body language displays, and what those displays mean to the client. Then she asks them, "Based on what we know about normal canine body language, is your interpretation valid?" Frequently, the answer is "no."

"I don't care if your dog wears your underwear," she says, "as long as he is healthy and not biting anyone." In other words, if your leadership position is not in question (and, as pointed out in chapter 12, your dog needs you to be a benevolent leader, so it's not necessarily a conscious effort on your part if you naturally fall into the role), interpreting your dog's body language can be left to you. But if you're encountering behavioral problems with your dog, you might want to consult an expert trainer or behaviorist to help you sort it out.

The body language we share with our dogs can be highly individual. "Each one of us has our own specific method of communicating with our pets," says Milani. "It is like a secret language."

It's a language that goes both ways. Our body language can communicate fear to our dog; it can communicate positive things as well. Try to be consistent with your body language, as well as your interpretation of your dog's body language. If your dog's language threatens you in any way, seek professional assistance.

Calming Signals

When Rugaas observed dogs interacting with one another, she identified twenty-seven different signals they use to avoid conflict and to maintain peace and quiet. She described these signals in her book, *On Talking Terms with Dogs: Calming Signals,* and video, *Calming Signals: What Your Dog Tells You.*

Once you're familiar with these communication signals, you'll spot them whenever you see dogs interact. A calm dog will use them with a fearful dog to let him know he means no harm. Two comfortable dogs might use them with one another to keep the peace. The next time you see two canines meeting for the first time, watch for some of these signals:

- looking away
- turning the head away from the other (which is done when looking away doesn't do the trick)
- yawning
- licking
- slow movements
- sitting and lying down, or freezing in place
- sniffing the ground
- approaching the other dog at a curve instead of straight on
- crouching in a play bow
- marking

Your dog might be using these signals on you, too! Once you're familiar with them, you can use them on your dog. If he is restless in the house, for example, try repeatedly yawning at him. He may let out a big yawn himself and lie down.

Turning away from a fearful dog should make him more comfortable. Curving in your approach rather than walking straight toward a dog will be more acceptable to a nervous dog.

Using calming signals is a way to communicate with your dog in universal dog language. "Go out and get yourself skilled at observing dogs, and you will see the next time your dog is telling you something—and you can do something about it," says Rugaas at the conclusion of her video.

Speaking Out Loud to Your Dog

I talk to my dogs all of the time—and not just baby talk and nonsense (though there's a little of that sometimes). I explain why I'm doing what I'm doing. When Kramer wants to go one direction on a walk, I'll tell him "we need to go this way because I need to mail a letter." He readily complies, and I believe he understands what I'm saying.

People who believe that their dogs understand only rudimentary commands, and therefore limit their verbal communication with their dogs to words they've been taught, are missing out. If you're verbal around your dog—and if you have an emotional connection to him—he's listening and comprehending a lot more than you think.

Susan McCullough of Vienna, Virginia, has long had a barking problem with her Shetland sheepdog, Cory. She's handled it through training, and putting him in a down stay, for example, when she was about to do something to trigger a barking fest, like opening or shutting the windows.

After learning more about animal communication and opening her mind to the possibility that dogs might understand more of what we tell them than she originally thought, McCullough tried her hand at explaining things to Cory. She got immediate results.

For example, Cory gets revved up when his owner takes the tablecloth off the dining room table (he's hoping for a game of "bullfight"). Recently, McCullough was clearing off the table, when Cory grew excited. She turned to him and said, "Cory, all I'm going to do is take off the newspapers and put away the placemats. Nothing else." To McCullogh's delight, he ceased and desisted immediately.

That's a single example from many where Cory calmed down and didn't bark when McCullough simply informed him of what's going on, explaining why it would be best for him not to bark. "I've been amazed at how well Cory seems to understand my explanations," says McCullough. "Doing this is making a big difference in our relationship: It's less stressful and more loving than it was before."

You might want to give it a try. It can't hurt. Even if your dog doesn't understand you, he probably enjoys your talking to him, and you may end up being surprised by the results.

Telepathic Communication

When I first learned that people were making money communicating telepathically with animals and relating what the animals said to their owners, I couldn't believe it. There's a sucker born every minute, I thought. But then, a few years later, at the urging of friends who'd had some remarkable experiences with animal communication, I tried it. I paid a professional animal communicator $35 for a half-hour session talking to Kramer and Scout. It was probably the most fun that $35 has ever bought me.

I wrote a magazine article about telepathic animal communication and took a couple of workshops on how to do it myself. When I was asked to write a book on the topic, I rolled up my sleeves and started talking with communicators and their clients.

I'm now a believer. Animals communicate telepathically with humans all of the time. As children, humans were told by their parents to close off that avenue of communication. ("It's just your imagination.") But if you open yourself to it, you can communicate without speaking to your dog (and receive communication from him).

Do you ever have a hunch that your dog wants something specific? Perhaps he sent you a message. Does your dog ever come up to you and just stare? I bet you find yourself getting up and getting something for him. You've probably just communicated with him telepathically.

My book *You Can Talk to Your Animals: Animal Communicators Tell You How* details many stories about animal communication and relates information from professional communicators about how to do it yourself.

For now, I ask you to be open to the possibility. When you have a feeling that your dog is saying something (if you're like me, you're always putting words in your dog's mouth), consider the possibility that you're receiving a telepathic message. The people I've spoken with who have opened their minds to this idea are thrilled with the results. It's a wonderful way to strengthen your bond with your dog.

If you're curious enough to try to communicate with your dog through a professional communicator, you can find one at the Web site of Penelope Smith, one of the pioneers in telepathic animal communication (www.animaltalk.net). Animal communicators primarily work over the telephone (using the phone to speak with you while they speak telepathically with the animal), so geographic proximity isn't important.

One of the great things about dogs is how they make their wishes known without language. Pay attention to your dog. Open your mind to everything he might be trying to tell you. Talk to him. He has a lot to say—if you listen with your eyes, ears, mind, and heart.

15 Safety First

Our dogs depend on us for everything. We control their food, water, exercise, even their elimination opportunities. We're also responsible for keeping them safe. There are a lot of hazards out there, and some are less obvious than others.

▸ DON'T PUT YOUR DOG IN DANGER ◂

When Rucey Myers of Seattle bought a smooth rubber ball for her three-month-old Labrador/Newfoundland mix, Jessie, the ball was just the right size for the puppy. But as the puppy grew (and the ball didn't), Myers discovered in a terrifying moment that the ball was dangerously small. When she tossed it to Jessie, she caught it, then tried to swallow it. The ball became stuck in the dog's throat. "I could see it, but since it was smooth and by then covered in spit, I couldn't get it out," recalls Myers. Luckily, the ball did not obstruct Jessie's airway, and Myers was able to rush her to the vet, who managed to extract it.

Inappropriate toys are among the many everyday objects and events that can pose a threat to your dog. It's not always possible to avoid all of life's hazards, but you can certainly take some precautionary measures to prevent placing your dog in danger.

Toys

Toys, as important as they are to dogs, can be dangerous. To avoid living the nightmare Myers experienced with Jessie, make sure any ball your dog plays with isn't small enough to choke him. If your dog is an aggressive chewer, be sure the toy can't be torn up into pieces that could be lodged in his throat, or be consumed and block his intestines. Supervise your dog after you introduce any new toy to make sure he doesn't play with it in a dangerous way. If he does, take it away. Regularly inspect any heavy-duty chew toys you leave your dog alone with to find any cracks or damage early on.

Collars and Tags Worn Around-the-Clock

When yellow Labrador retriever Harley was a puppy, a trainer told his owner, Susan Lennon of Rocky Hill, Connecticut, to leave his chain collar on him all the time. One day, Susan and Harley were in the bathroom together, and Harley was playing behind the toilet. Lennon heard a high-pitched squeal followed by a thump and discovered that her four-month-old puppy had hung himself by the collar on a fixture below the toilet. The collar was wrapped tightly around the metal fixture; Lennon's efforts at freeing him were futile. When she called 911, the dispatcher agreed to send an emergency unit only after Lennon threatened to kill herself if her dog died. Fifteen long minutes later, emergency personnel showed up and dismantled the toilet. Lennon had never been comfortable putting a choke chain on her dog, and that was the last day Harley ever wore one.

As this incident illustrates, it's not safe to leave a chain collar on a dog. If you use one for training, take it off as soon as you finish the session.

Tags can be dangerous, too. One day Susan Bemus looked out her kitchen window to see her golden/Lab mix, Digger, lying in a strange position, with her chin pinned to the deck. Digger's bone-shaped ID tag had slipped in the crack between two wooden slats, then turned 90 degrees. Digger was effectively tied with her neck to the ground. Luckily, Digger is a calm dog and didn't panic, so Bemus was able to rescue her easily. Bemus's dogs no longer wear collars when at home.

Paper Shredder

It may sound far-fetched, but paper shredders can also pose a real hazard for dogs. The type that automatically turn on when a piece of paper is inserted may also turn on when a dog licks it. Last spring, a Border collie named Recce licked a paper shredder and his tongue was pulled into the machine. Luckily, his owner was home and was able to rush him to the veterinary hospital. He survived despite an immense loss of blood and is learning to live with a partial tongue. If you have a paper shredder, keep it unplugged when you're not using it.

> **POOCH POINTER**
>
> **HOUSEHOLD HAZARDS TO DOGS**
>
> - *cleaning solutions*
> - *fertilizers*
> - *small toys that can become stuck in the throat*
> - *toxic plants*
> - *paper shredders that turn on automatically*
> - *chocolate*
> - *antifreeze*
> - *power lawn equipment*

Toxic Substances

Cleaning solutions, fertilizers, and toxic chemicals should be kept out of reach of inquisitive dogs. Dog-proof your home as you would childproof it for a toddler.

Some things that won't poison people can hurt dogs. The most notable example is chocolate, which contains a substance called theobromine; this can actually kill a dog. Don't leave chocolate out where your dog can get it.

An unexpected place your dog might encounter chocolate is mulch. Be sure that the mulch you buy for your garden isn't made from cocoa hulls.

Some houseplants can be toxic if eaten. If you have a dog who likes to munch on your plants, you'd better find a new home for plants like Boston ivy, philodendron, and amaryllis. An illustrated list of dangerous plants is available on the Internet at cal.vet.upenn.edu/poison/index.html.

Another dangerous substance for dogs is antifreeze, which can put your dog into kidney failure after he ingests even a trace amount. If you see a telltale green puddle, steer your dog clear of it, and be careful if you change your car's antifreeze. Look for pet-safe antifreeze, which is now available.

Tying a Dog Out

My pet peeve is something I see on a daily basis here in New York City. People take their dogs on errands, then tie them to a parking meter or fence when they go into a store. I don't get it. It's like leaving a baby in a stroller on the sidewalk. (Some European parents did just that in Manhattan a couple of years ago and were arrested for child abuse.) So many bad things could happen to your dog while he's waiting for you. Someone could steal him. He could get loose and run off. Another dog could come along and attack him. A child could approach your dog and poke him. Without you there to intervene, your dog might bite the child (and guess who would be blamed?). To me, it's not worth the risk. If I need to walk somewhere where the dogs aren't welcome, I leave them at home.

Another dangerous practice is tying your dog out in the yard. When you do this, particularly if he's unsupervised, you leave him vulnerable. Tying up a dog thwarts his flight instinct—when he feels threatened, there's nowhere for him to go. This can make many dogs behave aggressively toward perceived dangers, like people walking by, other animals entering the yard, or taunting children. It can do a number on your dog emotionally.

Not Identifying Your Dog

Letting your dog outside without an identification tag is courting danger. If he should escape from the yard or get away from you on a walk, his tag could be his ticket home rather than to a shelter.

When you travel with your dog, put a temporary ID tag on his collar, with the number where you can be reached, your cell phone number, and/or an emergency number. You can use a paper key tag, write on it with waterproof ink, and just tie it to your dog's collar.

Collars and tags do fall off. Other, less visible but more permanent means of identification are also available. A microchip the size of a grain of rice can be implanted between your dog's shoulder blades. When your dog is scanned at a shelter or vet's office, a number comes up. The person who scans it calls the chip's registry and is given your name. If you microchip your dog (which can be done at many vets' offices and shelters), be sure to register with a national database.

Keep your data at the registry up-to-date. It does your dog no good if the person who finds him can't reach you.

Another permanent identification method is tattooing. This is usually done on the dog's inner thigh, where there is less fur to cover it. A unique identification number is tattooed on the dog and, as with microchips, that number is registered with a national registry.

Car Travel Dangers

Think twice before taking your dog in the car with you on errands. The weather really should be cool, and not sunny, since cars can heat up quickly. By leaving your dog in the parked car, you also risk his escaping. This happened to a friend whose small dog wriggled out the crack he'd left in the window for ventilation. (He got his dog back.) Another possible danger is your car being stolen with your dog in it. Imagine how frantic that would leave you.

Take measures to secure your dog while you're driving. If you had an accident, your dog would be thrown. He might not only be hurt, but he could also become a canine missile and hurt the human passengers of the car. I use car-safety harnesses, which have a loop on the back through which my car's shoulder belt goes. If my car were large enough, I'd probably use crates instead.

Under no circumstances should you ever let your dog ride in the open bed of a pickup. An unsecured dog might fall out. One that is secured by a leash in the bed of a pickup might also fall out—and be left hanging from the leash.

Another common but dangerous practice is letting your dog stick his head out the open window while you're driving. Sure he loves it, but if you're traveling fast (and even if you're not), a piece of gravel could fly up and hit your dog in the face. He could be badly injured, even blinded. Would you let your child hang his head out the window of a moving car? Another possible danger is that if the window is open wide enough, your dog might actually fall out. This happened to the dog of another friend.

A final caution about car travel: If your car has passenger-side air bags, don't let your dog travel in the front seat. It's been well publicized that air bags, when inflated, are dangerous to children and small adults. Logic dictates that dogs would also be in danger of suffocation should the air bag be deployed.

Letting Your Dog Run Free

Some people let their dogs run loose in their neighborhoods. This happens more in suburbia and rural areas, but we have a neighbor in Brooklyn who does it. If you let your dog roam the neighborhood, you're exposing him to all sorts of dangers: being hit by a car, eating a poisonous substance, or being hurt by another animal. You're also alienating your neighbors by allowing your dog to eliminate indiscriminately on their property. Caring dog owners don't do it.

Other people take their dogs for walks on city streets but don't bother to leash them. They are confident that their dogs will not wander into the street. But dogs will be dogs, and most can't resist chasing small animals. It's a hardwired behavior. If a squirrel or cat should wander across the path of even the most well-trained canine, chances are good that the dog will give chase. That chase might take him in front of a car.

Another argument for not walking your dog off-leash on the sidewalk is that you might scare pedestrians who are afraid of dogs. Or you might encounter a dog-aggressive dog. Remember, your dog depends upon you to keep her safe.

Yard Dangers

Leaving your dog unattended in the yard all day can be dangerous. If your dog is an escape artist, he could be running around the neighborhood while you're at work. He could be stolen. Depending on your fence, another animal could enter your yard, where he could get into a scrap, or barrel into the fence by chasing a cat or squirrel. Assuming you dog-proof your house, your dog will be safer indoors when unattended.

Your yard offers dangers even when your dog is supervised. Yard work can be dangerous to her, since lawn mowers and string trimmers can cause pebbles and sticks to fly at high velocity. Your dog could sit or walk in the path of these flying objects and be hurt. You could prune a branch off a tree, and it could land on your dog. When you're paying attention to your work and not where your dog is, you're putting him in peril. Keep your dog in the house when you're using power equipment in the yard.

We owe it to our dogs to do everything we can to keep them safe. Before you decide to take your dog with you, think hard about whether he'll be safe. I'm not suggesting you be paranoid, but I do think it's worth thinking about the worst-case scenario and balancing the risks with the benefits of any situation in which you place your dog. Bad stuff happens, and if something bad should happen to your dog, you don't want to live with the guilt of knowing that it was you who put him in peril.

16 An Ounce of Prevention

Our dogs depend upon us to keep them healthy. They don't have the language skills to tell us when they feel bad, although if we observe them carefully enough, they can tell us in other ways. It's up to us to pay close attention, and touch our dogs regularly so that we can detect as early as possible when something's gone awry in their bodies.

▸ DON'T TAKE YOUR DOG'S HEALTH FOR GRANTED ◂

As with our own health, early detection is the name of the game with canine illness. "I tell people that if their dog doesn't feel well and isn't better within twenty-four hours, they should go to the vet," says Patrick Tate, D.V.M., a veterinarian in private practice in Webster Groves, Missouri. Tate points out that young puppies and elderly dogs—older than ten years—have fewer reserves, and so less time to spare. They should probably go to the vet as soon as they start feeling ill.

Even if your dog just doesn't seem right, call your vet. Tate describes a client who recently brought in her dog, saying that he hadn't been feeling right for a day. Tests revealed that the dog was suffering from autoimmune hemolytic anemia, an ailment that, if caught too late, is potentially life threatening. Detected early, it is easily treatable. Tate applauds the client's initiative in bringing in her dog so soon. "She knew her dog and knew to bring him in," he says.

Of course most of your dog's ailments won't be as dire, but little things can lead to real discomfort.

The Vaccination Debate

Annual vaccinations would, on the surface, appear to be the king of preventive care. But the notion that all animals should be vaccinated every year is starting to change. In the holistic community, vaccinations are generally seen as doing more harm than good.

Even some conventional veterinarians now advocate less frequent vaccinations. The Colorado State University College of Veterinary Medicine and Biological Sciences, for example, recommends a protocol of puppy or kitten shots, followed by a booster shot at age one year, then routine vaccinations only every three years after that. On its Web site (www.cvmbs.colostate.edu/vth/savp2.html), the school states that its rationale for this recommendation (as opposed to the traditional annual revaccination) "is based on the lack of scientific evidence to support the current practice of annual vaccination, and increasing documentation showing that overvaccinating has been associated with harmful side effects."

The holistic veterinarians I've consulted have blamed annual vaccinations, coupled with a genetic predisposition to a sensitivity to them, for the autoimmune disease that my eight-year-old Kramer has developed. I've been advised never to vaccinate him again.

Holistic vet Dee Blanco says that a single shot of a modified-live vaccine, given after the age of fourteen weeks, provides a lifetime of protection from illness. Continuing to jolt the immune system with more shots, she says, is not only unnecessary but counterproductive. "They don't do any good," she says. "They keep trying to stimulate, and just cause a confusion and an overload. This is often why there is autoimmune disease."

If you choose not to give your dog annual shots, don't forego his annual exam. Your dog needs to be given a thorough exam by a vet once a year. This provides the opportunity to ask questions, to do blood tests if your vet thinks they're necessary, and to have an expert eye observe your dog's health. The next time you visit your vet, ask about not giving shots this year. In this transition time, when recommendations are slowly changing, it might be something your vet agrees with but doesn't bring up unless you mention it.

Instead of vaccinating against a specific disease, you can ask your vet to draw blood for a special test called a titer, which measures the antibodies in the blood and indicates whether your dog is protected. The trouble with titers is that they may tell you your dog is not protected even if he is. The antibodies don't have to be circulating in the blood in order for them to be present and kick in when exposed to the disease. However, if you decide not to vaccinate, a titer that tells you your dog is protected can give you great peace of mind.

If you feel you must vaccinate, consider getting separate vaccinations, spaced at least a couple of weeks (or even a year) apart, for each of the diseases you're trying to protect your dog from. This will mean a smaller jolt to the immune system than the big 5- or 7-in-1 combination shot that is typically given.

Jean Dodds, D.V.M., a noted immunologist, hematologist, and researcher on the effects of vaccines, says that the only "clinically significant" diseases that adult dogs should be vaccinated against are distemper, parvo, and rabies. The other diseases—covered by what she calls the "combo-wombo" shot—are either too mild, if contracted, to merit vaccinating against, are rarely seen today, or the vaccine is relatively ineffectual (the leptospirosis shots, for example, cover only a few of the many strains of lepto). The efficacy and side effects of the Lyme disease vaccines are a matter of controversy.

Conventional Versus Holistic

After Kramer became ill with autoimmune disease, I discovered that there are two different mind-sets within the veterinary community about how best to treat a pet. Kramer happened to come down with something that conventional veterinarians have no real treatment for (besides suppressing the immune system). Autoimmune disease, in which the body's immune system mistakes its own tissue for a foreign substance and attacks it, is something conventional vets cannot cure; rather, they can control the symptoms through immunosuppressive drugs, to keep the immune system from attacking the body.

When Kramer was diagnosed, my conventional vet suggested that I look into alternative veterinary approaches, for example, homeopathy, herbs, acupuncture, and traditional Chinese medicine, to see if I could find help for him. I am forever

▼ POOCH POINTER ▼

DIFFERENCES BETWEEN CONVENTIONAL AND HOLISTIC VETERINARY MEDICINE

In general, the differing approaches of conventional and holistic veterinarians can be characterized this way:

A holistic veterinarian:

- *looks at the whole animal, not simply symptoms*
- *seeks to find the cause of the illness and cure it, even if symptoms temporarily grow worse*
- *takes longer in treating*
- *tends to avoid vaccination*
- *tends to avoid the use of antibiotics*
- *frequently advises feeding a fresh-foods diet*
- *is more likely to charge by the hour*

A conventional veterinarian:

- *treats individual symptoms*
- *tends to see different symptoms as separate conditions rather than part of the same illness*
- *provides more immediate relief of symptoms*
- *tends to encourage vaccination (though some conventional vets are starting to recommend less frequent vaccination)*
- *prescribes antibiotics more readily*
- *usually encourages feeding commercial diets*
- *is more likely to charge for the services rendered*

grateful to her for that, since one year later, Kramer's health has substantially improved through homeopathy and nutritional therapy. I'm a convert.

A big difference between holistic and conventional veterinary medicine is that holistic practitioners tend to look at the whole animal, try to ascertain the cause of the ailment, and then treat the cause. Conventional vets tend first to address symptoms. As a pet owner, the conventional approach can be attractive, because it means that your animal is provided quicker relief. Holistic vets argue that by suppressing symptoms, you're pushing the illness deeper into the animal, and more serious illness could result.

Our homeopathic veterinarian, Dee Blanco, stresses that treating all symptoms of an illness as soon as they appear isn't healthy. "Health is never about never getting ill," she says. "You should go through an illness, purge your system, and feel better." A healthy immune system can fight illness, so the best preventive medicine, she says, is that which builds and fortifies your dog's immune system. Blanco feels that annual vaccinations, monthly parasite preventives, and commercial dog foods do the opposite.

The best way to maintain good health in your dogs is to:

- feed her a fresh, whole diet
- serve her fresh, filtered water
- minimize exposure to assaults on the immune system, like vaccinations, chemical-parasite preventives, lawn chemicals, and cigarette smoke
- give your dog plenty of appropriate exercise in a clean environment

If you choose, as I have, to treat your dog holistically, that doesn't mean ignoring your dog's symptoms, though chances are good that your dog will become ill less frequently. It's still your responsibility to pay close attention to how he's feeling, and to consult your veterinarian when you fear a problem. Your holistic vet may well choose not to immediately alleviate the symptoms. But as the symptoms might point to a larger illness, it's important to talk to your vet about them.

If you consult with your holistic veterinarian by phone, you're well-advised to have a local vet to whom you can take your dog in an emergency. This vet can be the eyes and ears for your remote vet. My local vet is happy to explain, slowly and clearly, what she's seeing as she examines my dogs, so that I can relay the information accurately to my homeopathic vet.

Parasite Prevention

Ticks and fleas are the bane of your dog's existence. They can make you and your dog miserable. Before the 1990s, dog owners typically dealt with fleas only after they had an infestation on their hands. They employed flea baths, flea dips, flea collars, and even flea bombs for the house. These involved a lot of chemicals, which didn't even work that well. Ticks were dispatched manually.

There's a new generation of flea and tick preventives available, all of which are more effective. "We are at the best point we have ever been on in preventing fleas," says Tate. Topicals like Advantage and Frontline, applied between a dog's shoulder blades monthly, actually kill the parasite. (Advantage works for fleas only, while Frontline works for fleas and ticks.) An oral flea preventive, Program, interrupts the flea's reproductive cycle, though it doesn't kill the flea. Another monthly oral product, Sentinel, combines Program and Interceptor, a heartworm preventive that also fights other worms. Revolution, a megacombination product introduced in 1999, prevents fleas, ticks, heartworm, and other parasites, like ear mites.

Heartworm preventives are typically given monthly (though daily heartworm preventives are available) to prevent your dog from contracting heartworm, a potentially fatal disease transmitted by mosquitoes in which worms take up residence in the heart and pulmonary arteries. The treatment for heartworm disease used to employ arsenic and was hard on the dog. Milder treatments are now available.

Are these products really necessary? It depends on where you live and even on your dog's attractiveness to parasites. If fleas aren't a problem for your dog, then you probably don't need to load him up on chemicals. "I tell people if you don't need it, don't use it," says Tate. But, he adds, if you've never been through a real flea or tick infestation, you can't appreciate how awful it can be. If fleas are a problem in your area, you'll avoid an infestation if you give the preventive during flea season.

Holistic practitioners generally caution you to avoid giving any unnecessary chemicals to your dog. We stopped using monthly flea and tick preventive after Kramer was diagnosed with lupus in 1999. His immune system was compromised, so I avoided (and continue to avoid) all possible insults to it. At the same time, we switched to a fresh-foods diet. So far, no fleas and only one tick in the last eighteen months. I credit that as much to Kramer and Scout's diet as anything else—though they're city dogs, they're exposed to fleas and ticks on a daily basis in the tall grasses of the vast city park they run around in every day.

Keep Those Teeth Clean

Dental disease is prevalent among dogs. Studies indicate that by the age of three, 80 percent of dogs show some signs of oral disease. You can do much to prevent dental disease. If you do a good enough job, you can avoid anesthetizing your dog for teeth cleaning.

Just as you brush your own teeth, you can also brush your dog's teeth to help keep her mouth healthy. Buy some toothpaste made especially for dogs—it comes in such appetizing flavors as poultry and liver. My dogs think it tastes great. Remember, don't use human toothpaste; the foaming agents might upset your dog's stomach. It can get tricky getting your dog accustomed to toothbrushing, but every little bit helps. The inside of the teeth (the tongue side) are difficult to brush, but don't worry about them—food doesn't tend to stick there.

If brushing seems too daunting, there's a simpler solution: bones. Give your dog a fresh, raw bone (like a marrow bone) to chew on, suggests Tate. Bones are healthy for dogs, and they do a great job of cleaning their teeth. The bone should be the appropriate size for your dog. Don't feed her a bone she could easily swallow whole. The idea is for her to spend some time chewing. I always supervise my dogs when they're chewing bones, because I wouldn't want them to break off a little piece and choke.

What about rawhide? Fresh bones are safer, since rawhide may have been preserved and cured with toxic chemicals. I know from experience that rawhide can be swallowed in large pieces—in past years, Kramer swallowed some frighteningly large pieces. The danger is that the rawhide could choke your dog or cause an intestinal blockage. Another fear is the source of the rawhide: if you buy beef bones intended for human consumption, you don't have to worry that they're from a source that might carry mad cow disease. (See chapter 17 for more information on feeding bones as part of your dog's diet.)

Check Those Ears!

Veterinarian Tate sees many dogs who come in with uncomfortable ear infections. Many infections can be prevented by proper care of the ears. "The best way I know to prevent ear infections is to look at the ear on a regular basis," Tate says. Examine your dog's ears regularly, and look for discharge, swelling, or redness. Get into the habit of sniffing your dog's ears. Know what a normal ear smell is, and let your vet know if you detect a yeasty or otherwise abnormal odor.

Your vet can describe the best way to clean your dog's ears. My holistic vet recommends olive oil (just to clean the earflap, not inside the ear canal). Some vets recommend commercial preparations.

If your dog is constantly scratching at her ears, she might have an allergy. Talk to your vet about detecting what she might be allergic to so you can make her more comfortable. It's always better to find a solution to the source of a problem rather than to treat only the symptoms.

Lumps and Bumps

Part of your regular examination of your dog should include rubbing his body and detecting any lumps or bumps that might have sprouted. If you find one, contact your vet. "Lumps and bumps are not to be ignored," says Tate. Your vet will probably want to aspirate the lump, which means sticking a needle into it and examining the material he draws out. There's a good chance that the lump will turn out to be nothing. But if it is something serious, like cancer, you'll want to have it removed right away. The earlier you catch a malignant lump, the better the chance it can be surgically removed before the cancer has spread.

Sometimes what at first touch feels like a bump is actually a tick. It's important to catch ticks as soon as possible after they land on your dog. Tick-borne diseases, like Lyme disease and Rocky Mountain spotted fever, are transmitted only after the tick has been attached for some hours. If you examine your dog every day and remove any ticks you find, you help to eliminate the chance that the nasty insect will transmit disease to your dog. Be sure to protect your hand with gloves or a tissue before grabbing a tick.

No matter how you treat your animals—and you may change your thinking about this over the course of your dog's life—your dog is better off if you detect any problems early. By examining his body regularly and paying close attention to any signals he's sending you, you do more than simply keep him healthier: You also promote a stronger bond between the two of you. I'm no longer embarrassed to tell my vet that my dog is just "a little off." I don't care if it turns out that there's nothing wrong with him—in fact, I hope they'll find nothing wrong, and that whatever ails him will pass swiftly. But if there is something wrong, I want to know right away so that I can begin treatment.

17 Food: You Get What You Pay For

Remember that expression "You are what you eat"? The basis of good health, for dogs, humans, you name the species, is good nutrition. The commercial dog foods marketed today all say that they are "complete and balanced," but that doesn't mean they're all alike. There are real differences between the various foods. Better ingredients tend to cost more, so a good rule of thumb is that the more expensive the food is, the better it is.

More and more dog owners are feeding their animals a home-prepared diet rather than relying on commercial food for good nutrition. They're educating themselves and providing fresh, nutritious, and balanced food for their dogs. For the dog owner who is willing to put in some extra time and effort to promote her dog's health, a fresh-foods diet can really pay off.

▸ DON'T UNDERMINE YOUR DOG'S HEALTH WITH POOR NUTRITION ◂

If you choose to feed your dog a commercially prepared diet, buy the best food you can afford. Bear in mind that higher-quality ingredients are more digestible, which means that your dog's body uses more of the nutrients. While the premium foods might be more expensive, your dog will get more out of them, and you'll be able to feed him less food. The suggested feeding portion on the dog food's label is the amount of food your dog must eat to meet his nutritional requirements. That's why less expensive foods suggest such large portions.

Commercial Dog-Food Brands

How do you know a food is good? Read labels. First, identify the food's primary source of protein. Grains are a cheap source of protein found in most dog foods. The trouble is, dogs are built to eat and digest meat, not grains. Yes, there are some predigested grains in the stomachs of the killed animals wolves eat. But it's hard to imagine a wolf out in a field gorging himself on corn or wheat.

Meat is a better, more natural (and more expensive) source of protein for dogs. Look at the label. Meat should be the protein source. Ingredients are listed in descending order, by weight. Look for meat to be prominently featured among the first few ingredients.

Second, look for ingredients you can understand. Just as with the packaged foods you buy for yourself, you don't want dog food that's loaded with sugar, dyes, and preservatives. "Stick to foods that have few nonfood things in them," advises Patrick Tate. "The fewer number of ingredients, the better."

Third, familiarize yourself with what some of the meat-related terms on the label mean. Whole-meat products are listed by just the name of the meat ("chicken," "lamb," or "beef," for instance). By-products are derived from the rest of the animal after the meat has been taken away (not including hair, horns, teeth, or hooves). With poultry by-products, the law requires that they not include feces or foreign matter, "except in unavoidable trace amounts." Meat meals are rendered animal tissue. The Animal Protection Institute, an animal advocacy group, advises against buying food that relies on meat meals and by-products.

Now that you know what to look for, you might be surprised when you read the label on your package of dog food. To make it easier for you to comparison-shop, visit the "Dog Foods Comparison Chart" Web site, compiled by Earl Wolfe, at home.hawaii.rr.com/wolfepack/. It lists the ingredients of more than one hundred types of dog foods, including well-known and readily available commercial brands, as well as independent and special-order brands. You may find some brands you've never heard of. Web site links, where available, are provided for each manufacturer, and offer a wealth of information. I've found that this site's URL sometimes changes, but if I do a search under "dog foods comparison chart," it always pops up.

> **▼ POOCH POINTER ▼**
>
> **WHAT TO LOOK FOR IN A DOG-FOOD LABEL**
>
> *If you are feeding your dog a commercial diet, here's what to look for (and to avoid) on the label:*
>
> *Look for:*
>
> - *meat sources listed as two of the first few ingredients*
> - *whole-food ingredients, like vegetables and meats*
> - *human-grade meat (with USDA in front of the type of meat)*
> - *fewer ingredients*
>
> *Avoid:*
>
> - *grains as the main source of protein*
> - *meat meals and by-products*
> - *ingredients you don't understand*
> - *artificial preservatives, like BHA, BHT, and ethoxyquin*
> - *added sugar*
> - *dyes*

What's Actually in Dog Food?

The label doesn't tell the whole story. Even if you select a food whose label lists the best ingredients you can find, it will still lack optimal nutrition. Vitamins and enzymes are lost in the heat processing of the food, which is why the companies have to add vitamins (they're listed on the label) to make the food nutritionally complete.

The big question is the source of the meats. When you look at exactly what goes into your dog's commercial food, you might become squeamish. For example, in her book, *The Consumer's Guide to Dog Food,* author Liz Palika writes: "In the majority of states, it is legal (and common) practice for pet-food manufacturers to use what are known as '4-D' meat sources: animals that are dead, dying, diseased, or disabled when they arrive at the slaughterhouse."

I know that when I served commercial food to my dogs, I didn't want to think about what was in it. But if your curiosity gets the better of you, or if you're thinking about switching to a fresh diet, consider reading the investigative report from the Animal Protection Institute, called "What's Really in Pet Food." You can find it on the

World Wide Web, or ask for a free copy by mail. See the Resources section for the URL and contact information.

Another exposé on what goes into pet food is Ann Martin's book, *Foods Pets Die For,* which reveals, among other things, that the pet-food industry has turned our companion animals into cannibals: Pet food routinely contains meats from dogs and cats.

Preparing Homemade Food for Your Dog

Commercial dog food is certainly easy. So is pouring a bowl of cereal for yourself and calling it a meal. But while most of us aren't willing to subsist on a diet of breakfast cereal whose added vitamins and minerals meet the daily requirements, many *are* willing to ask our dogs to spend a lifetime eating the equivalent.

Picture, if you can, a child who has eaten nothing but breakfast cereal. Now contrast that mental image with a child who eats a variety of fresh vegetables and protein sources every day. Which do you think would be more healthy, more vibrant? That same contrast exists between dogs who eat nothing but commercial food and those who are fed a fresh, raw diet. Dogs who are fed fresh, whole foods don't merely survive, says Dee Blanco, but "they flourish. It is the difference between health and subsistence." Blanco lists good nutrition as the cornerstone of preventive veterinary medicine.

When Kramer became ill with autoimmune disease and I sought holistic care for him, I began to realize that what I really needed to do was to change his diet to provide him with optimal nutrition. I was feeding him a top-of-the-line commercial food, but because he had a delicate digestive system, any variation of his diet resulted in a flare-up of the inflammatory bowel disease he'd been diagnosed with. He would suffer from diarrhea and vomiting, and be a very sick dog.

Then I switched to a fresh-foods diet. I initially cooked the food and then gradually switched to an all-raw diet. (I do cook sweet potatoes for him, so that I can mash them, and on the infrequent occasions I include grains, I cook those, too.) The difference in Kramer is astounding. Yes, he is also being treated by homeopathy and with a synthetic thyroid hormone. I think it's the synergy between the three things (homeopathy, medicine, and good nutrition) that has done the trick. He's a vibrant dog now, has lots of energy, and looks great. A year ago, at the age of seven, Kramer looked like an old dog. Today, at eight, he seems like a young dog.

Gina Barnett of San Francisco, who feeds a raw diet to her Great Dane/ Labrador mix, Fred, has never had to deal with major illness with him. But she has clearly seen improvements in his health since putting him on a raw diet. When Barnett adopted Fred from a shelter as a young adult dog, he had a history of ear infections and the ubiquitous skin problems so many canines experience. Those problems disappeared completely through feeding him a raw diet. "His coat is thick and glossy, and he no longer has itchy paws, dry flaky skin, or a waxy discharge in his ears," Barnett says. Moreover, Fred rarely gets sick. His owner takes him to see her homeopathic vet for his annual well-dog checkup and estimates that she's spent four hundred dollars in veterinary bills on Fred in the last four years.

"I do not mean to imply that a raw diet is a panacea for every canine ailment," she says. "But, as with human health, optimum nutrition is the foundation for any successful treatment, whether conventional or holistic."

The Basics of Home-Prepared Diets

Entire books are devoted to home-prepared diets, but basically, here's how I feed my dogs: Their current diet consists of raw ground meat, ground fresh vegetables, cottage or ricotta cheese, sometimes some extras like mashed sweet potatoes or some kind of grain or pasta, and several nutritional supplements suggested by our holistic vet to address specific health problems. Twice a week, they eat raw, meaty bones, like turkey necks or chicken backs. It's not complicated or difficult. It is, apparently, delicious. Dry kibble doesn't begin to compare, judging by Kramer's reaction to the fresh food. (Scout will enthusiastically eat anything.)

I buy organic vegetables at the health-food store, which doesn't sell meat. I buy the meat at the grocery store. I know organic meat would be better, but I take comfort in the fact that I'm feeding them meat sold for human consumption, unlike the meat that goes into kibble. I enjoy the control I have over what my dogs eat.

Risks

When I tell people that I feed my pets a raw diet, they invariably ask about the risks of raw meat. I explain what's been explained to me: The dog's digestive tract is shorter, and food spends much less time going through. In addition, their system is more acidic, so bacteria doesn't have a chance to flourish. "Your pet's digestive system has evolved over two million years to eat raw meat," writes Kymythy Schultze in her book *Natural Nutrition for Dogs and Cats: The Ultimate Diet.* She points out that the best defense against bacteria is a healthy immune system, which a raw diet promotes.

When I tell folks that I feed my dogs raw poultry bones, they blanch. I explain that raw bones, which are healthy for the dogs, are soft, and can be chewed up without event. "Remember the species of animal you are feeding," writes Schultze. "Its entire digestive system is designed to eat raw meat and bones, including bird bones."

I've never had a problem on either count. That's not to say that no one has. I know this may be a risk, but it's one I'm willing to take because the health benefits are so great.

Before feeding your dog a raw diet, educate yourself. Weigh the benefits and the risks. It's a decision only you can make.

Will I Do it Right?

The commercial pet-food manufacturers have done a pretty good job convincing pet owners that they couldn't possibly know enough to feed their dogs properly. Yet, we're trusted to feed ourselves and our children. Sure, dogs have different nutritional needs from people. But all it takes is some research to learn about your dog's nutritional needs. Then you can apply that knowledge to a fresh diet, just as you do to your own. I would not advocate starting a home-prepared diet without first doing research. After all, you're trying to help your dog.

The Internet is also a great source of information, though, of course, you should weigh everything you read on it against established sources of information. If nothing else, Internet mailing lists can put you in touch with people who are feeding their dogs a home-prepared diet, so you won't feel alone. That really boosted my confidence.

Who Has Time?

The idea of taking the time to prepare your dog's food fresh every day is daunting. But it's not as time-consuming as it may sound. "For me, the raw diet is

▼ POOCH POINTER ▼

SOURCES OF INFORMATION

Several books are staples on the bookshelves of people who want to learn about home-prepared diets for their dogs.

- Dr. Pitcairn's Complete Guide to Natural Health for Dogs and Cats *by Richard Pitcairn, D.V.M., Ph.D., and Susan Hubble Pitcairn*
- Give Your Dog A Bone *by Ian Billinghurst, B.V.Sc.*
- Grow Your Pup with Bones *by Ian Billinghurst, B.V.Sc.*
- Natural Nutrition for Dogs and Cats: The Ultimate Diet *by Kymythy Schultze, C.C.N., A.H.I.*
- Reigning Cats and Dogs *by Pat McKay*

All of these are available from Dogwise, the on-line and mail-order bookstore (www.dogwise.com).

actually easier than feeding processed commercial food," says Barnett. "I no longer worry about running out of kibble or making trips to a specialty pet store to buy food. I shop for Fred's meat, fruit, and vegetables at the farmers' markets and grocers where I buy my own food." Barnett feeds Fred one meal a day, and says that it takes her ten minutes or less to chop his raw veggies in the food processor, add supplements, and dish it up with the raw meat portion of his meal.

Another option is to work in advance. Susan Lennon feeds two meals a day to her Labrador retriever, Harley. One meal comprises turkey necks or chicken wings. The other is a mixture of pulped vegetables, raw meat, and eggs, which she makes ahead of time and freezes. Lennon says it takes her a couple of hours every two weeks to make these patties, and no time at all to thaw and serve.

Feeding a fresh-food diet takes a little more planning on my part, and I find it a bit more time-consuming than scooping kibble out of a bag, but the benefits to my dogs' health and the enthusiasm with which the meal is received make it worth it to me.

Deciding what to feed your dog has long-term implications for his health. If you have the time and inclination to feed him a fresh diet, you'll doubtless see a difference in your dog. "The benefits are so many," says Blanco. "The joy that you see in your dog. The joy that you feel in your heart. The fact that you, not some big corporation, are controlling the ingredients."

If you're not ready to feed a home-prepared diet, Blanco recommends supplementing kibble with a portion of what you're eating for dinner (assuming that you eat healthfully). "Cook a little extra for your dog," she suggests. Your dog will enjoy the variation in his diet (eating the same thing every single day is torture for him, Blanco asserts). Since the kibble is already balanced, don't let his diet be more than 25 to 50 percent fresh, or you'll risk throwing the diet out of balance.

When you select kibble, read the label judiciously, and find the highest quality you can get for your dog. He'll thank you for it.

18 Good Grooming

Grooming your dog is about more than good looks. Sure, a well-groomed dog is more enjoyable to look at, but regular grooming is also important to your dog's comfort and health. Mats pull at the skin and hurt. Dirty dogs feel itchy and uncomfortable.

Different dogs have different grooming needs, depending on their coat. But even if your dog is a sleek greyhound, you should give him a regular once-over with your eyes and fingers to keep tabs on his coat and skin condition. At a minimum, all dogs need regular toenail trimming (unless the city sidewalks take care of that), and should have their ears and teeth checked regularly.

DON'T LET GROOMING TURN INTO A CHORE

If your dog is a nonshedding dog with a continuously growing coat, you know the importance of regular, professional grooming. But no matter how much money you shell out at the groomer, you must spend a certain amount of time brushing your dog and ensuring that she's mat-free and comfortable.

Grooming shouldn't be a chore. If you do it regularly, it should be a pleasure for you and your dog, because you're not doing anything to her that should be painful. If you seldom groom your dog, or if she is only groomed when she's sent

▼ POOCH POINTER ▼

SHEDDING AND NONSHEDDING BREEDS

Big shedders:

- *Alaskan malamute*
- *beagle*
- *Belgian sheepdog*
- *Belgian Tervuren*
- *Bernese mountain dog*
- *borzoi*
- *collie*
- *corgi*
- *dalmatian*
- *Doberman pinscher*
- *German shepherd*
- *golden retriever*
- *keeshond*
- *Labrador retriever*
- *Saint Bernard*
- *Samoyed*
- *Siberian husky*
- *smooth fox terrier*

Minimal shedders:

- *Bedlington terrier*
- *bichon frise*
- *Bouvier des Flandres*
- *Chinese crested*
- *dachshund*
- *greyhound*
- *Maltese*
- *poodle*
- *schnauzer*
- *Scottish terrier*
- *shih tzu*
- *soft-coated wheaten terrier*
- *Yorkshire terrier*

to the groomer, she'll dread grooming sessions, since they'll take a long time and consist of lots of hair-pulling. If you're like me, you remember your mother combing out tangled hair. It hurt! You don't want that to be a part of your dog's relationship with you or your groomer.

One of the most important grooming decisions should be made before you acquire your dog: If you can't stand a lot of dog hair around the house, you might be interested in a nonshedding breed. But there's a trade-off to having a dog that doesn't shed: that dog's hair grows continuously (like human hair), and must be cared for properly. This means on top of professional grooming, he'll need in-home grooming. If you don't have time for this kind of coat hair, maybe a shorter-haired breed is right for you.

If you already own a longhaired dog, be realistic about the amount of hair you're willing to take care of, suggests Laura Watts, a professional dog groomer in Charlotte, North Carolina. If you don't want to do a lot of grooming, don't keep your dog in a show cut. I shudder to think about how much work it takes to maintain a standard poodle in a full show cut, for example (although I admire people who can do it). Kramer and Scout are kept in a short kennel clip.

Watts explains that some coated breeds (like a cocker spaniel) have been bred to have increasingly profuse coats in order to be more impressive in the show ring. If you buy such a breed from show lines, be prepared for a profuse coat. Have your breeder show you how to properly care for that coat, including proper brushing.

Start Early

You'll do yourself, your dog, and your groomer a favor if, from the moment you get him, you condition your dog to having his body touched. If you acquire your dog as a puppy, and you start showing him that having his body touched is a pleasant feeling, he won't develop a fear of being handled. A dog that is not opposed to being touched has a much better time at the groomer (and being groomed at home).

Start slowly: Have some treats handy, and lift up your dog's foot. Then give her a treat. Next, lift up her foot, and spread her toes; then give her a treat. Pick up her foot, spread her toes, and gently pull on her toenails. Then give her another treat. Keep this routine upbeat and brief. Similarly, condition her to let you look in her ears, look at her teeth (including the back teeth), and touch every part of her body. "You are teaching your dog to enjoy being handled," Watts explains.

Besides helping you to groom your dog more easily, this conditioning helps your dog whenever she has to be handled by a dog-care professional. Even dogs who never go to a professional groomer must be seen at the vet's office.

Use the Right Equipment

There's a dizzying array of grooming equipment out there. One of my favorite sources for grooming supplies is the "New England Serum" catalog. It's important that you buy the right equipment for your dog, and it's also important for you to know how to use it. If you bought your dog from a breeder, she can teach you how to groom your dog. Otherwise, ask a professional groomer for at-home grooming advice. They're wise to supply it, since it will make their job all the easier.

At the least, you'll need an appropriate brush and comb, shampoo, toenail clippers, and perhaps a mat-breaker, conditioner, and nail file. Before we brought Kramer home, I went to the pet-supply store and bought him a brush. The rubber currycomb I purchased was completely wrong for a poodle (a slicker brush is more appropriate). I should have sought some professional advice before heading to the store, because the unknowledgeable store clerk wasn't able to help me. Without the right type of brush, grooming efforts can be ineffective.

The Importance of Toenail Care

Most dogs must have their toenails clipped to keep them from growing so long that they interfere with how the dog's foot touches the ground. Active dogs who walk on concrete or asphalt may not need such regular trimming, since the nails can be worn down. It's such a pleasure not to hear toenails clicking on the floor.

Again, early intervention is the best way to get your dog accustomed to having his nails trimmed. Make it as happy an experience as possible. Some dogs just hate it, and will put up a fight. Many owners leave the job to a professional (a groomer or veterinarian). If you choose this route, make sure you take your dog in often enough to keep her nails short.

The thing that's tricky about nail trimming is that the quick, which is inside dogs' toenails, grows *with* the nail. On humans, it's easy to cut long nails, because the quick always ends at the top of our fingers. We can also see the quick. But if you cut your dog's long toenail short, you will surely cut into the quick. This is not only painful for your dog, but it also fosters a bad association with the toenail trimmer. If your dog has light-colored nails, you can see the quick. If your dog's nails are black, you must cut just a little at a time. If you look carefully, you can see a little white spot when the quick is near.

When you trim your dog's nails, the quick recedes. So if your dog's nails have become long, you'll need to trim them regularly just a little bit at a time. Eventually, you'll have a short nail you can keep short.

Some dog owners use a grinder, or Dremel, to grind rather than trim their dogs' nails. This can be effective but should only be done by a professional or by a dedicated dog owner who has been carefully trained by a professional, says groomer Watts. Grinding your dogs' nails too short can do more damage than clipping them too short, she says.

Don't forget the dewclaws! Some dogs have them, the extra toenails up near the dew pad partly up their legs. They're the doggie equivalent of thumbs. Some breeds are born without dewclaws, and some breed standards call for the dewclaws to be removed when the puppy is young. Some breeds, like the briard and beauceron, even have double dewclaws on their hind legs.

If your dog has dewclaws, it's important to keep them trimmed short. Since dewclaws don't come into contact with the ground, they won't be worn down naturally. Long dewclaws can catch on grass or brush and rip, which can be painful. Worse, neglected dewclaws can grow so long that they curl around and dig back into the flesh. If your canine has dewclaws, keep a close eye on them, and don't let them get long. They should be a part of your dog's weekly examination.

Checking Other Parts of the Body

Your weekly grooming/examination session should include looking inside the ears. Look for redness, inflammation, or excessive discharge. Smell them regularly so that you can detect any early signs of infection. Talk to your vet about the best way to clean your dog's ears, as well as how regularly they should be cleaned.

You should also keep an eye on your dog's teeth. Gum disease is rampant among canines. If you're not giving your dogs fresh bones to chew on (see chapters 16 and 17), you should be brushing your dog's teeth regularly to keep them clean. Gum infections can be particularly dangerous for older dogs, so pay close attention to the color of your dog's gums; look for redness or puffiness.

Catching Problems

One of the main benefits of regularly handling your dog through grooming is that you will pick up slight changes in his body. Brushing and rubbing your dog allows you to examine his coat and his skin. You'll feel lumps and bumps before they grow large. Discuss anything that worries you with your veterinarian. Coat and skin changes can indicate serious problems within your dog's body (like thyroid problems), so it's important to monitor them.

Watts had a melanoma removed from her Doberman while it was still a spot on his skin. She was so familiar with every inch of his body that, as she was examining his skin, she picked up on it even before it was a lump. Early detection can be vital in treating cancer, so this grooming process is also an important preventive health measure.

Regularly examining your dog can also help you to catch nasty ticks. If you're not using a tick preventive, you should examine your dog daily for ticks during tick season, since the insect must be attached for at least twenty-four hours before it transmits Lyme disease.

Bathing

How often should you bathe your dog? "When she starts to smell bad," Watts says. If you find that your dog needs a bath more often than she used to, mention it to your vet.

Bathing doesn't have to be a traumatic experience. We bathe our poodles in the bathtub, using a special hose purchased for the purpose. It attaches to the shower. Its nozzle lies flat against the dog's coat, which allows a thorough rinsing.

Doggie bathtubs are now available to make bathing less of a chore. The Booster Bath, made by Paws for Thought, is a portable plastic tub on a pedestal, which gets an enthusiastic thumbs-up from Ann Daugherty. She bathes three Samoyeds in it. "I love it!" she says.

Selecting a Professional Groomer

"It is a leap of faith when you take your dog to the groomer," admits Watts. It can be scary to leave your dog somewhere without being able to witness what happens to her there. Most grooming shops prefer that you drop off your dog in the morning and pick her up in the afternoon—owners aren't usually welcome to watch, since it can interfere with the groomer's work. Watts says that of the dogs whose owners have stayed with them, one or two have behaved better in the owner's presence, but most are better behaved without their owners on hand.

Watts advises interviewing potential groomers in advance. Ask to see the facility, and inquire about sanitizing procedures. Ask what would happen if the dog were to become ill or injured on the grooming table. ("In order to cut hair, you have to use sharp scissors and clippers; sometimes accidents happen," says Watts. "Even the best groomer in the world occasionally has accidents.") See how the groomer interacts with the dogs in his care.

Trust your instincts. Even if the groomer has immaculate facilities and says all the right things, if you're not comfortable with him, don't leave your dog there. "Always trust your gut," Watts says. If you take your dog in for a second grooming at a shop, and your dog is resistant to going in, pay attention to that signal; ask the groomer about how your dog behaved the last time he was groomed. The groomer's answer can reveal a lot about her attitude toward your dog. Again, follow your gut.

Even if you use a professional groomer, your dog still needs you to check her regularly. "A really big owner responsibility is to put their hands on their dog on a regular basis," says Watts. "Thoroughly check her out."

Building Your Bond

Like bathing, grooming your dog doesn't have to be a chore. If you do it regularly, it can be a pleasant time. Handling your dog in a loving manner feels good to both of you. Just ask Daugherty, who grooms her three double-coated dogs once a week: "In addition to keeping my dogs looking and feeling great, the time I spend grooming them affords me some intimate, one-on-one time with each dog. When I set up my grooming table, my three Samoyeds all start doing the 'pick me' dance, each hoping he or she will be the first one chosen for some special table time with Mom."

Here's your chance to spend some quality time focusing on your dog. For both of you, it can be a loving oasis in a busy week.

19 Dogs Belong with Their Families

Dogs are pack animals. Their ancestors, wolves, traveled in packs. When we acquire a dog, we become his pack. Dogs need time with us—it's part of their genetic makeup. When you force your dog to live away from his pack, you're not only making him miserable (and asking him to find his own ways to entertain himself), but you're also missing out on the wonderful companionship a dog can provide.

▸ DON'T BANISH YOUR DOG TO AN OUTDOOR LIFE ◂

Whenever I see a dog who lives outdoors all of the time—in summer or winter, rain or shine—I wonder why the owner even bothers to have a dog. Dogs excel at keeping us company. When you're in the presence of a canine, you're not alone. They enjoy our company as much (if not more) than we enjoy theirs. So why exile a dog to his yard? If you want to spend time with your outdoor dog, you have to make a special effort. When your dog lives in the house, you can spend time together just by living.

In the U.S. penal system, an inmate's worst punishment (aside from death) is solitary confinement. Yet, that's just what we subject our dogs to when they're kept alone in the yard. "Solitary confinement makes people crazy, why wouldn't it make a dog insane?" asks pet-care columnist Gina Spadafori.

Why do people leave their dogs in the yard? Some people were brought up to believe that dogs belong outdoors. For them, it's inconceivable to think of a dog in their house. Others banish their dog because he's not fully housetrained, or perhaps he's destructive. Through the use of humane confinement indoors, however, a canine can be easily housetrained and taught to chew only on appropriate items.

When you leave your dog alone all day in the yard (or even with a canine companion) you're asking for trouble. "It's not fair to ask an intelligent pack animal to live alone in a backyard and do nothing all day. It's not possible for him to do that," Spadafori says. Your dog will have to entertain himself somehow to relieve the sheer boredom. The result? Barking, digging, fence jumping, or destruction. "He's just got to get the ya-yas out," Spadafori believes. "It's what he has to do to maintain his sanity."

Indoor-Outdoor Dogs

Even if your dog spends time indoors with you when you're home, he's better off inside the house when you're away from home. If he's not completely trustworthy, confine him. (See chapters 2 and 10 for more information on confining and crating.) But if he's indoors, he's less likely to bother neighbors with his barking and, in general, he's safer. (See chapter 15 for information on backyard hazards.)

Dog trainer Sue Sternberg of Accord, New York, feels that leaving dogs in the yard gives them too much freedom. "I think that when I leave my dogs out, I'm just allowing them to run amok, which can lead to behavioral problems. They're like wild animals on their own out there. They're making up their own rules." Indoors, it's quieter, and there are plenty of distractions, she notes, so there's less to bark at. "Indoors means sleep rather than play and bark."

Spadafori's dogs have what she considers an ideal situation: a dog door. They can go in and out as they please. They're not barkers, so she doesn't worry that they'll disturb the neighbors when she's not home.

We have a yard, but Kramer and Scout are never in it unsupervised. Its fence is wrought-iron and quite short—only 4 feet high. If they wanted to, the dogs could jump it (though they've never shown an inclination). I'm more worried about someone either opening the gate or actually stealing them. So our dogs—confirmed indoor pets—stay in the yard only for a few minutes at a time, and always have a human watching them. Most of their outdoor time is spent on their walks.

If you have a yard but no fence, be judicious about tying your dog out. While this practice is better than letting him go untethered, it's not a good idea to leave a dog tied out unsupervised. When a dog is tied out without a fence to protect him, he's vulnerable to anyone or anything that enters the yard. If a dog is tied, he knows he can't run. If he is frightened and can't run away from the object of his fear, he has no choice but to lash out. (It's the old "fight or flight" rule.) Tying your dog out is a good way to get her hurt, and make her aggressive. It's safer for dog owners without a fenced yard to put their dog on-leash and walk him.

If you're outside with your dog and can protect him, a tie out can be a good way to let your dog keep you company as you garden (assuming you're not using power tools, which can be dangerous).

Dogs Who Prefer the Outdoors

I realize that some dogs love being outside. Northern breeds, in particular, just love the great outdoors, especially when it's cold. Chugach, an Alaskan malamute owned by Stephen Peters of Marquette, Michigan, made his preference for sleeping outdoors clear to his owner. Chugach recently succumbed after a long fight with cancer, and Peters kept him indoors as he was healing from surgery. When he was healthy enough, Chugach spent a good deal of his time outdoors; Peters joined him if the weather was nice. He'd ask to come inside every night about 9:15, and then the two would go for a walk. Chugach would get his bedtime biscuit, and then head outside.

The malamute also stayed outside during the day while Peters was at work. He was in a secure 25- by 8-foot run that had a doghouse on one end and a shade over the first 8 feet, so that he could get out of the sun without going into the doghouse.

This preference for being outdoors is not uncommon among Northern breeds, says Peters, who lives in a very cool climate. "The Northern breeds like to be as cool as possible at any time of the year. Malamutes have special 'circuitry' to keep them warm in cold weather, but it does not kick in until temperatures get to about 35 degrees below zero. Anything warmer than that, and their normal coat will do quite nicely," Peters explains.

Chugach would ask to come in when it was raining ("he seemed to think that malamutes would melt in the rain") and, of course, for meals.

The crucial difference between dogs like Chugach and those who always live outdoors is that Chugach was a true member of the family. He was invited indoors whenever his owner was home. He was kept outside during the day, because Peters felt he was happier there. The two spent quality time together. Chugach's outdoor time was his choice.

If you have a dog you feel prefers the great outdoors, spend ample time with him, either indoors or outdoors. You need to make sure he gets his exercise, and that you take him for walks. This way, his territory can expand beyond his borders. Dogs are territorial, but they like their territory to grow, says Spadafori. They like to see new things. So it's important that you don't limit your dog to your yard.

"Certain breeds are quite happy outdoors," Spadafori says. "but that's no excuse for ignoring their need for family."

Watchdogs

If you keep your dog in the yard in order to deter unwanted visitors, think how much safer you'd be if your dog were in the house with you. If you're worried about intruders, keep a large dog-food bowl in the yard. Such a practice provides a warning that a dog is around. But if someone were able to get into your house, you'd feel a lot better with your dog standing between you and the intruder than you would if he were out in the yard. "What good is a protection dog if he's out in the yard?" asks Spadafori.

Bringing the Outdoor Dog Inside

If you've been keeping your dog outdoors and have a change of heart about it, rest assured that you can transform him into an indoor dog. Many formerly outdoor dogs are adopted to new homes as adults and successfully make the transition into indoor life. If your dog isn't completely housetrained, consult chapter 2 for information on that process. If you're worried he'll be destructive, chapters 2 and 11 provide information on crate training and confinement. They also discuss chew-toy training, which can keep your dog from chewing up your belongings.

Chloe, an Irish setter (a breed not known for its watchdog abilities), spent at least three years tied up outside a vacant home in Norman, Oklahoma. Her owners had moved without selling the home, and left Chloe behind to guard the house.

Concerned neighbors took the setter away from this lonely existence and, with the permission of her former owners, Chloe was adopted by Lavinia Kay Frank.

This onetime outdoor-only dog immediately became a convert to the wonders of living inside. She joined Frank's two other dogs and seamlessly made the transition to indoor life. The only remnant of her past is her occasional reluctance to venture out in the yard alone. Frank has to put Chloe on-leash and walk her out to the patio to pee before she leaves for work in the morning. "When I put the lead on her, she knows we'll *both* be coming back inside," Frank suspects.

Just imagine how desirable a warm house full of people must be to an outdoor dog on a cold winter's day. When I see dogs that are kept outside, I think about how much they must yearn for a little snuggle time on the couch with their owner. Your dog will be happier and safer indoors, and he'll provide you with what he's best at: great companionship. If you're not enjoying that now, you don't know what you're missing.

20 Spay or Neuter Your Dog

If you're considering the possibility of breeding your dog (or profiting from your male dog's stud services), please consider a few facts.

Thousands of dogs are killed every day in animal shelters simply because nobody wants them. In our society, it seems puppies are brought into this world only to be killed. It's a national tragedy you contribute to if you breed your dog outside of an established, responsible program. Even if you find homes for your dog's puppies, you're contributing to the problem, because the homes you find are those that could go to other animals.

DON'T LET YOUR DOG BREED (EXCEPT UNDER IDEAL CIRCUMSTANCES)

I can hear your objection: "But I have a purebred dog. She has papers." Even owners of purebred dogs shouldn't breed their pets unless it is part of a carefully planned program to further the breed.

Breeding your sweet golden retriever with the neighbor's golden simply won't do, given the current pet overpopulation crisis. If you want to breed your animal, you should run a series of genetic tests to make sure that your dog won't pass any health problems on to her puppies.

A Breeder's Responsibilities

If you want to become a breeder, you should satisfy the requirements mentioned in chapter 1. Everything said there about a good breeder should apply to you—which isn't easy.

Genetic tests are just the tip of the iceberg. A good breeder has done research and carefully selected the breeding partner for the dog in order to create a litter that exemplifies the breed's best and healthiest traits.

"A good breeder breeds only the best to the best," says Gina Spadafori.

Responsible breeders make a serious commitment to the puppies they breed. "They have to be responsible for these lives that they bring into the world," says Chris Walkowicz, a longtime breeder first of German shepherds, and now bearded collies.

As a responsible breeder, you promise to take into your home any puppy you've bred for any reason, any time. "You have to understand that eight years from now, somebody might get a divorce and call you and say 'I have no home for Buster, will you take him back?'" The answer to that question must be yes, says Walkowicz. It's part of the commitment you make when you decide to breed.

You can ensure that your dog is worthy of breeding—that is, exemplifies what is best about the breed—by showing your dog and having her win titles. Knowledgeable puppy buyers know that this is the hallmark of a good breeder.

If you compete in conformation shows, where your dog is judged solely on the basis of how she conforms to the breed standard, she can earn the title *Champion.* Most pedigrees of well-bred dogs are littered with the initials *Ch.* before the dog's ancestors' names.

Finishing a championship isn't a prerequisite for breeding, says Walkowicz, but any dog you consider breeding should prove herself in the competitive arena that interests you. That might be obedience, herding, lure coursing, or any one of a number of activities. The point is, the dog should excel in something, as well as being a good, healthy example of the breed.

Breeders should be dedicated to the breed, not to their individual dog, Walkowicz says.

Rescue

Many breeders also participate in purebred rescue groups, whose members help individual dogs of their favorite breed. If a purebred dog shows up at a shelter, the purebred rescue group for that breed takes the animal out of the shelter, evaluates the dog, and provides foster care while looking for a good home for him. This is a way for breeders to give back to their breed.

Breeding Is Expensive!

Some people get dollar signs in their eyes when they think about breeding their dog. But the truth of the matter is, when breeding is done right, there's little money to be made, despite the fact that responsible breeders can and should get top dollar for their puppies. A good breeder is lucky to break even, Walkowicz points out.

Mary Lynn D'Aubin of Scottsdale, Arizona, has two Labrador retrievers, Ike and Babs. D'Aubin was considering breeding Babs and so hadn't spayed her. Her husband was reluctant to neuter Ike (a reluctance not uncommon in human males). They went to great effort to keep the two dogs apart during Babs's heat cycle.

But there's little stronger than the will of an intact male dog when he's around a bitch in heat. D'Aubin came home one day to find that Ike had broken out of his crate and through a sliding glass door in order to join Babs in the backyard. Babs gave birth to nine puppies, two of whom were stillborn.

D'Aubin calculates that, with Babs's prenatal veterinary visits, shipping the last puppy to his new home, and everything in between, she spent $1,400 on routine expenses every breeder would doubtless incur, and another $2,100 in transportation and medical expenses. She earned $1,850 on the sale of the puppies.

"I lost about $1,650 on this litter," D'Aubin says. "Granted, there were a number of unusual expenses, and I covered costs that most [breeders] wouldn't have, but some of the costs I absorbed are not out of line for ethical breeders."

The costs go beyond the monetary—to the emotional. "One cannot factor in time, caring, sleeplessness, heartache over sick/dead puppies, anxiety, and working full-time and caretaking the rest of the time," she says. The messy puppies also put a strain on her marriage.

However, puppies also bring a lot of happiness. "The pure unadulterated joy in those little lives is so awesome, it hides the costs somewhat." D'Aubin spayed Babs after her litter was born, but she says she would consider breeding again—but only after more careful planning. "No more accidental breedings!"

Spaying and Neutering Are Good for Your Dog

If after reading this chapter you don't feel you're up to the commitment or expense of breeding, you can take great comfort in knowing that spaying or neutering is actually good for your dog. It's not only the right thing to do (under almost all circumstances), but it's also the healthy thing to do.

Consider this: A female dog that is spayed before her first heat greatly reduces her chances of getting mammary (breast) cancer. If you spay your dog before her

▼ POOCH POINTER ▼

THE BENEFITS OF SPAYING OR NEUTERING YOUR DOG

- *Your dog won't contribute to pet overpopulation.*
- *Neutered dogs tend to be less aggressive.*
- *Territorial marking is reduced.*
- *Chances of testicular and ovarian cancers are eliminated.*
- *Chances of prostate and mammary cancers are reduced.*
- *The urge to mate is eliminated, and the inclination to roam is reduced.*
- *No need to fend off suitors when a female is in heat.*
- *No staining from a female in heat.*

first heat, her relative risk of breast cancer is .05 percent. If she goes through one heat cycle, that risk is 8 percent. Let her have two or more heat cycles, and she has a 26 percent chance of getting breast cancer, according to data supplied by the AKC's Canine Health Foundation. Spaying, during which the uterus is removed, also eliminates the risk of uterine cancer, as well as the chances of uterine infection, which is not uncommon in intact females.

Neutering your male eliminates the chance that he'll get testicular cancer; it reduces the possibility of prostate cancer and prostate enlargement. A neutered male is likely to have fewer fights, which is also better for his health.

Behavioral Advantages

Frankly, I have a hard time imagining living with an unaltered dog. A neutered male is much less likely to be the target of negative attention from other dogs. In the off-leash park we visit, it's common for an unneutered male to be greeted with a snarl when he joins a group of dogs.

Unneutered males are more likely to act aggressively in general. Most fatal dog attacks involve unneutered adolescent males, says pet expert Spadafori. A neutered male won't go on the single-minded quest for the bitch in heat. As the D'Aubins' Labrador, Ike, illustrates, that inclination is difficult to thwart. Intact males can become amazing escape artists.

Neutered males mark less (though certainly neutered males and even females do mark their territory—but not as often in the house), and they don't spend their time being sexually frustrated.

If it's the look of a neutered male that troubles you, you're in luck. You can now buy Neuticles, testicular implants that your vet can insert to make your neutered male look completely intact.

Unspayed female dogs are more aloof and moody, says Spadafori. "They go through PMS just like we do," she says. When Spadafori put an end to the show career of her flat-coated retriever, Heather, and had her spayed, she was amazed at the change in her dog's disposition. "She's a lot sweeter, a little bit clingier, and a little bit more loving."

While it's never too late to neuter your dog (I know people who had to have their fifteen-year-old Lab neutered due to testicular cancer), the earlier it's done, the easier it is on the dog. Vets have been neutering puppies as young as eight weeks old for more than a decade, and have not discovered negative effects later in the dog's life. Such early spay and neuter is one way shelters can release puppies and kittens to new homes and know that they won't be receiving their offspring a year later.

Estimates vary on the number of dogs annually euthanized in our country. I've seen figures as low as 1.5 million and as high as 15 million. Whatever the exact number, it's too many. Be a part of the solution, and do the right thing: Spay or neuter your dog.

21 Keep Up with the Times

It can be challenging to raise a dog. If you're a caring dog owner, you want the best for your dog. You know she's depending on you for everything. Part of the challenge is that the current thinking—the most acceptable way to do things with and for your dog—keeps changing. Don't let the evolving philosophies frustrate you. View them as an opportunity.

Dogs are being treated more gently than ever. They're being recognized as thinking, feeling creatures. They're truly becoming part of the family. We owe it to our dogs to keep abreast of current thinking and not be satisfied to do things the way our parents did, just because it's familiar. Dog training and veterinary care are evolving. Stay on top of the changes. It's easier now than ever before to do that.

▸ DON'T STOP LEARNING ◂

In 1992, when Kramer joined our family as a puppy, I read books, talked to experts (the vet, trainer, and knowledgeable dog owners), and did the best for him that I could. Eight years later, I do almost everything differently from what I did in 1992. The one constant has been my abiding love and concern for his well-being.

Back then, I vaccinated him every year, fed him dry kibble, walked him with a choke chain, gave him antibiotics at the drop of a hat, even tried doing an alpha roll (where I would roll him on his back to show him I was the boss), and scruff shake (where I would grab him by the scruff of the neck and growl in his face) when he misbehaved. I was following advice I'd been given. Most of it felt bad to me.

Now, I feed him a healthy home-prepared diet with nutritional supplements; no longer vaccinate except where required by law (after years of annual vaccinations, he has a lifetime of immunity, my holistic vet assures me); use a flat collar; train him with a clicker and treats; care for his health homeopathically; and hardly ever yell at him, let alone physically punish him.

What happened? Did I change? I think of it as evolving. I have my own research and the Internet to thank for my evolution. I subscribe to a number of Internet mailing lists, populated by knowledgeable dog people and professionals. These lists have allowed me to keep up with current thinking in health care and training for my dogs. I have a place where I can ask questions and learn from others' experiences.

The result is that I'm treating my dogs more gently and spend much less time being frustrated with them. They're happier, I'm happier, everybody wins. If I were stuck in my 1992 mentality, I'm convinced, I'd have less healthy, more neurotic dogs.

How to Stay Abreast

Where can you keep up with the ever-changing thinking on dog training, behavior, and health? Reading books like this is a start. As is subscribing to and reading dog magazines and newsletters (see Resources).

But it's the twenty-first century, and the Internet is king. It's the place to go for up-to-the-minute information and to "meet" people who have been through the various situations you seek help on.

The Internet

First, a warning about the Internet. Be discerning about the information you gather here. Unlike books and magazine articles, which usually go through several layers of review before publication, the Internet is full of information that may have little basis in fact. Read everything with a grain of salt, and look for supporting information. One of the nice things about Internet mailing lists is that after you subscribe for a while, you can get to know the people a little who post messages and judge whether they're knowledgeable. After some time, you develop a trust with these "virtual friends" (and actual strangers, since you probably have never met). Then it's like taking advice from a trusted ally.

Internet mailing lists are a kind of electronic bulletin board. Each individual list is set up to bring together people with a common interest. Send a note to the list, and everyone who subscribes to it receives your note in their E-mail (or posted to a Web site if that's how they prefer to read it). It's a great, immediate way to receive lots of information, as well as a wonderful way to belong to a virtual community.

Mailing lists exist for most dog breeds, and they're frequently specific in the interest addressed. For example, there's a list for setter owners who feed raw diets to their dogs. There's a list for owners of shy dogs. There are any number of lists for owners interested in natural health care for their animals. I'm on a list for dogs with immune problems.

There are also some wonderful, more general lists, like canine-1 or critter-chat, which simply supply a means for people who love dogs to talk about them. They address more general interests or a wider variety of topics.

There are several ways to find an Internet mailing list that suits your needs. One is to go to e-groups at www.egroups.com. Do a general or specific search (for example, "epileptic dogs"), and the appropriate lists come up. With a couple of clicks of the mouse, you can subscribe. Other dog-related mailing lists can be found at www.k9web.com/dog-faqs/lists/email-list.htm.

Once you subscribe to a list, you'll receive a welcome message from the list owner and probably be urged to introduce yourself. You sometimes have to send a message confirming that you want to subscribe (to prevent people from subscribing you to a list you're not interested in).

A mailing list is what you make it. Some people, "lurkers," read but don't post to the list. That's fine. Others are frequent posters. I post on some lists and lurk on others (depending upon whether I have anything useful to say). The mailing lists I stay on don't allow "flame wars," whereby people get into nasty E-mail arguments. When flaming begins, the list owner usually comes down on the offenders.

Be forewarned: These lists can be very time-consuming. Depending on the volume (and number) of the lists to which you subscribe, you might receive hundreds of messages a day. In my E-mail program, I set up folders for each list I'm on, and ask the program to automatically sort the incoming messages into the folders. That helps to keep the messages from becoming unmanageable.

Internet newsgroups, which are accessed via a newsreader, are open to the public and tend to be more of a free-for-all. Anyone can access a newsgroup and post there. My attempts at getting dog-related information from newsgroups haven't been terribly successful. The information I've found has tended to be general and oriented toward the new dog owner. But I'm sure others have had much more success.

To use newsgroups, go to your newsreader and search for the topic you're interested in. Like mailing lists, there are general, as well as specific newsgroups.

Anyone with Internet access can put up a Web site. Thousands of dog-related sites are available to peruse. The trick to finding good sites is using a good search engine (my two favorites are www.google.com and www.askjeeves.com). Subscribers to mailing lists also frequently post the addresses for good sites they've found. Again, bear in mind that most Web sites have not gone through a review process, so be sure to verify the information you find on them. Web sites that are put together by reputable organizations carry more weight, in my opinion, than those put up by individuals. In the anonymous world of the Internet, a Web site with an authoritative-sounding name could actually be written and run by a thirteen-year-old.

Conferences

As wonderful as the Internet is, it's no substitute for face-to-face contact with people. Several dog-related conferences bring together experts and allow interaction with the dog-owning participants. Several groups sponsor such conferences. Check out the following Web sites to see if there's a conference near you:

Puppyworks (www.puppyworks.com). The single most valuable conference I think I've attended was Puppyworks's "Holistic Healthy Dog Conference," in 1999. It changed the lives of my dogs and me.

The Association of Pet Dog Trainers (www.adpt.com), an organization that promotes positive training methods, holds a national conference every year for trainers. The public can attend (for a fee). In conjunction with the conference, the organization puts on a terrific trade show—open to the public—which features training equipment. The conference moves around from year to year. APDT's Web site also lists events sponsored by other organizations.

Legacy by Mail (www.legacy-by-mail.com), trainer Terry Ryan's organization, offers a variety of workshops, as well as a behavior and training camp.

Dog Camps

Dog camps are springing up around the country. These camps, where you can vacation with your dog, are not only a great way to bond with your dog, but they can also present a lot of valuable information.

Your time spent at dog camp is a rare week where all the attention is focused on the dogs, their needs, and enjoyment. Each camp offers athletic events, such as agility and flyball, training, and, frequently, lectures on dog care. Here are just a few: Camp Gone to the Dogs in Vermont; the Dog's Camp in North Carolina; Camp Winnaribbun in Nevada; Dog Scout Camp in Michigan; and Dog Days of Wisconsin in, where else, Wisconsin.

I have a special reason for mentioning dog camps as a source of information. Kramer and I attended Camp Gone to the Dogs in 1998, and had a great time. I've often written about that camp and have spoken with many people who said that what they learned at camp changed the way they treat their dogs' training and health care. And what a fun way to learn!

Thanks to the Internet, staying on top of the latest information on what's best for your dog isn't hard. There's no reason to make decisions for your dog based on decades-old information, nor do you have to take advice from your hairdresser whose neighbor "raises" dogs. Keep your eyes open for new sources of information, and don't stop learning. You and your dog have so much to gain.

22 The More the Merrier?

Acquiring a canine companion for your dog can be a wonderful idea. Dogs are pack animals, and if you have to leave them alone all day, the company of a canine pal might make the time pass more quickly and pleasantly. But it's not a situation to enter into lightly. Two dogs can be more than twice the work of one. And if you're getting a dog in the hopes of fixing behavioral problems you're having with your current dog, you might just end up with two ill-behaved dogs on your hands.

▸ DON'T ADD ANOTHER DOG WITHOUT SERIOUS PREPARATION ◂

Before you add a dog to your household, make sure you've thought about the extra work and expense. You'll have twice the training and grooming, twice the food and supplies, and twice the veterinary and boarding costs. Make sure you are strong enough to handle both dogs on-leash, and that your bank account is strong enough to handle the added expenses.

Be sure you're adding the dog for the right reasons, which include having extra love to pass around. In our household, two dogs and two humans is the perfect ratio. There's always a free hand available to scratch a canine head or belly.

There are also a lot of wrong reasons to add a dog. Don't get a second dog because you don't have time for the first. If you don't have time for one, you certainly won't have time for two. Don't add a second dog just because you feel guilty about leaving your pet alone.

Don't add a dog so you won't have to exercise the dog you already own. "A second dog is not a substitute for sufficient outdoor exercise," says Robin Kovary, a New York City–based dog trainer and behaviorist, and director of the American Dog Trainers Network. "A second dog might make a great playmate, but both dogs will require daily outdoor exercise to keep them happy, healthy, and well behaved." (See chapter 9 for more information about the importance of exercise.)

Don't bring a new dog into your home if you are having behavioral problems with your existing dog. "Your first dog should be obedience-trained and fully housebroken before you bring in another dog," Kovary says.

Take the time to modify any problem behavior before you bring in another dog. Adding a second won't solve behavioral problems; in fact, it might double them. "You wouldn't want your dog teaching a puppy a behavior that drives you nuts," says Char Bebiak, head trainer/behaviorist for Ralston Purina Co. "Then you have two dogs doing it."

Before bringing home another dog, make sure your dog is emotionally ready for a permanent playmate. Look closely at his behavior. How does he interact with other dogs? Does he like to play? Is he properly socialized? Is he accepting of dogs in his own home? Invite some of his playmates over to make sure he's comfortable with having other dogs around. If you can answer "yes" to the above questions, then your dog might well be a good candidate for a new brother or sister.

If you tend to spoil and pamper your dog, and he sometimes challenges you, adding another one to the mix might be courting trouble. Your dog will likely be threatened by the newcomer and be unwilling to share you. Get your relationship with your dog squared away before adding another.

Choosing the Second Dog

Choosing a second dog is much like choosing your first. The same considerations of time, breed preferences, and lifestyle apply. Look at chapter 1 to help you consider some of your options.

If possible, your dogs should meet before adopting the new dog. Carefully watch their reactions to one another.

The big difference in adding a second dog is that you're making decisions relative to your first one.

Gender

Should you add a dog of the same or opposite sex of your resident dog? As a general rule, dogs of opposite sex—provided that they are neutered—are the best match. The worst match is two unneutered males.

Size

The two dogs shouldn't be so different in size as to cause possible injury to one another. For example, a Yorkie might have a hard time with the addition of a mastiff.

Age

Should you get a puppy or an adult dog? Your resident dog might be more accepting of a puppy, but he also might become exhausted by a youngster. You know your dog best; try to imagine whether a puppy would breathe new life into him or turn him into a crabby old dog. If you decide to get a puppy, remember that they tend to be more work for the human family members than adult dogs.

An adult dog might seem like a greater threat to your dog, but if you bring them together gradually and work hard to avert jealousy by paying a great deal of attention to your first dog, your transition should be smooth. While adult dogs can have the disadvantage of your not knowing their background, many seem so grateful to find themselves in a good home that they bond instantly and make great pets. This was certainly the case with Scout.

If your dog is elderly—that is, more than nine years old—you might reconsider adding a dog, says Bebiak. Turning his life upside down could be detrimental to him.

Introducing the New Dog

When it's time to bring your new dog home, introduce the two on neutral ground if possible. This reduces the chance for territorial behavior on the part of your dog ("this is *my* yard!"). Then, walk home together.

Bebiak favors keeping your resident dog off-leash during the introduction period. If you can't find any neutral territory, where your dog can be safely off-leash, she recommends introducing the dogs in your fenced yard. If you don't have one, use your imagination. Perhaps you could borrow a friend's yard or an apartment.

Have your resident dog off-leash in the yard (or other location), and bring the new dog in on-leash. Let them sniff and greet, and praise them both like crazy. As leader of the pack, you should set the tone for the meeting. By keeping the encounter upbeat, you can reassure your first dog that the newcomer is a good thing.

Once the initial greeting and explorations are over, bring the second dog into the house, and put her into her crate. Let your resident dog come in, see, and smell her so she'll be safe in the knowledge that the new dog isn't taking over the house.

▼ POOCH POINTER ▼

BE PREPARED

Each dog should have his own food bowl, water bowl, and toys (including chew toys and plush toys). Your new dog will also need his own collar and leash. Each should also have a crate, which is an essential tool for helping separate the dogs. It gives them their own space, and the first dog some time to be alone, by himself, or with you.

Before bringing your new dog home, put away all the toys, so that there's nothing for either dog to be possessive about, Kovary suggests.

Over the course of the next two to four weeks, bring the dogs together slowly, under supervision. This is tough advice to follow, because it's hard to muster the patience to keep the dogs apart.

When you bring them together, read the dogs' signals, and separate them if there's any tension or aggression. "They will have a whole lifetime together, so why rush them?" Bebiak asks.

Living with Two Dogs

When you add a dog, your primary dog should maintain his primary status. He needs reassuring that his relationship with you hasn't changed. Feed him first, pet him first, give him treats first. Share some time alone together. Kovary suggests that when visitors come to your home or greet you on a walk, ask them to pet your primary dog first, which helps to keep him from feeling displaced.

The second dog should earn privileges, Bebiak says. Don't give her all the fringe benefits that the resident dog has earned. Make her earn them herself.

While you should initially maintain your first dog's primary status, if the second dog emerges as the dominant personality, don't try to change the natural order of things by favoring the first dog, or by reprimanding nonviolent dominant behavior. "Intervening only disturbs the natural balance," Kovary says. "You cannot make a dominant dog subordinate to a subordinate dog." If you try, you'll end up with two unhappy dogs, as well as the potential for fighting.

Watch for any sign of hostility, and pay close attention to body language. Be careful not to put the dogs in situations that can spark an altercation over food, toys, or even human family members. Feed the dogs separately, each with his own food bowl and water bowl. They should also have separate beds, crates, and toys. After the transition is complete and the two dogs are getting along famously, they may care to share toys, which is fine. My dogs share a water bowl as well, but I always supervise them when they're eating—Scout steals Kramer's food if she thinks she can get away with it.

When you can't watch them together during those first few weeks—even if you just leave the room to answer the phone—keep them apart by using baby gates, exercise pens, or crates. You don't want an unexpected altercation.

New Problems

Even with these precautions, you might see some brand-new behavioral problems in your first dog. If he's feeling ignored, he may misbehave in order to get your attention. "He may act out as a way to say, 'are you still paying attention to me?'" Bebiak says. In this situation, soiling the house is not unusual for even the most faithfully housetrained dog.

The jealousy is natural, and should dissipate with time, if you remember to give both dogs plenty of love and each some special time alone with you.

Watching your dogs become accustomed to one another and turn into fast friends is a thrill. It's worth the effort to do it right.

The decision to add a dog to your household has a long-term impact on your family dynamics and your pocketbook. Plan ahead, make sure you're ready (and that your dog is ready as well), and give both dogs the time and space they need to get to know one another.

Two dogs are twice the love and twice the fun as one. They're also twice the trouble. There are eight muddy paws to wipe instead of four; two dogs' worth of poop to scoop instead of one; twice the toenails to clip; and two leashes to untangle.

But two dogs also mean two tongues to kiss you, four eyes to gaze at you lovingly, and two bellies to rub. That can definitely be worth the extra effort.

23 Kids and Dogs

Dogs and kids make a great combination. Many of us have fond memories of growing up with a loving childhood dog. Whether you're adding a baby to a family that already includes a dog, or adding a dog to a family with kids, you need to take steps to ensure that the kids and dogs live together happily—and safely.

▸ DON'T FORGET TO PREPARE YOUR DOG FOR YOUR NEW BABY ◂

If your dog has long been a member of your family, she's used to your constant attention, and playing adult-type games with you, like wrestling on the floor and tug-of-war. When a new baby joins the family, the rules change. Behaviors that were allowable when your dog did them to you—like jumping up, mouthing, and licking—may seem inappropriate after the baby arrives.

That's why you need to prepare your dog ahead of time. "The notion of the baby coming home and the dog instantly loving it is what we all hope for, but if you don't inform the dog ahead of time, it can be a confusing time," says dog trainer Sarah Wilson. "Making some changes ahead of time can make it so much smoother for all concerned."

Wilson recommends, for example, that you change your praise words if you, like many people, call your dog "good boy" or "good girl." Start telling him he's a "good dog" instead. Otherwise, when you tell your baby, "Oh, you're such a smart boy!" the dog might well come running over and stick his head in between you and your infant. If you scold him, he'll be completely confused. "I think a lot of things that people sometimes label as jealousy are actually confusion and stress on the dog's part," Wilson says.

If your dog jumps up on you, leaps into your lap, climbs up on the couch without being invited, or grabs items out of your hands, you'll need to change the rules before the baby arrives, Wilson says. "It doesn't have to be an unpleasant process. It can be positive." When your dog understands the new rules, you won't experience these difficulties after the baby arrives. You can imagine, for example, how unpleasant it would be for you, your dog, and your baby if your dog were to jump into your lap with the infant already there.

Introducing the New Baby

I've always heard that prior to bringing home the baby, new parents should bring home a hospital blanket the baby's been sleeping on, so that the baby's scent will be familiar to the dog. I asked Wilson whether that was good advice. "I don't see how it could hurt," she replied. "But I also don't see any particular plus." Instead, Wilson says, it is a better idea for the mother or father to sleep with a baby blanket one night, and then wrap the baby in that blanket when she is brought home from the hospital and introduced to the dog. The canine will then recognize that the new little bundle has a familiar scent and is therefore part of the family.

When you introduce the dog and baby, Wilson advises having one adult handle the dog, on-leash, while the other parent holds the baby. Your dog will probably be curious about the new baby. He'll want to look and sniff her. "Stay relaxed and sound relaxed, but be ready in case the dog gets too curious and wants to stuff his nose down the diaper," Wilson says. You can then say "leave it," and call the dog away. (This assumes that you've taught your dog the leave it command, which is usually part of any training class.)

What you don't want to do, says Wilson, is stand next to the dog, hold your breath, and chant rapidly, "It's okay, it's just a baby; it's okay, it's just a baby."

Since dogs take their cues from us, such nervous chanting tells your dog that this is something you're concerned about. "You want to be relaxed and happy, praise the dog, let him know that this is a wonderful addition to all of your lives, that this is nothing to be worried about."

How Will You Care for Your Dog?

Before the baby arrives, make plans to ensure that your dog will still get the exercise she needs. You'll be exhausted and sleep-deprived, but it won't do you (or your dog) any good to have an underexercised dog underfoot. Arrange for a friend or neighbor to walk your dog, or have someone sit with the baby while you and the dog take a walk and share some quality time. A friend could stroll with you and hold your dog's leash while you walk with the baby. Depending on your dog and your baby, you may be able to walk both at the same time, but don't count on it.

When Barbara O'Rourke of Lakeport, California, gave birth to twin girls nine years ago, she wished she'd prepared herself and her boxers, Archie and Beau. "I was overwhelmed with fatigue, poopy diapers, and nonstop feedings," recalls O'Rourke. "I am sure my dogs felt excluded, confused, and hurt during those first few months." Friends and neighbors offered to help out the new mother, and, looking back, O'Rourke wishes she'd accepted their aid and arranged for them to walk the dogs with her while she walked the babies. (She found walking the two dogs with the twins' stroller unwieldy and impossible.) But after the babies arrived, "I couldn't even begin to think about anything but getting through the day."

O'Rourke advises other dog-owning couples to plan—before the baby arrives—for how the dog's needs will be met during the first few hectic months after bringing home baby. "You would never forsake your human children when you brought home a puppy," she says. "Don't forsake the pups because you brought home a baby."

Childproofing Your Dog

A crate is an essential tool for any dog living with a child. It's imperative that you not leave your dog and baby or toddler alone together, so you'll need to separate them. You'll doubtless have a playpen for your child, and the crate serves as a playpen for your dog. You'll not only be able to crate your dog when necessary, but your dog will also be able to crate herself when she needs to take a time-out. Teach your child that the dog's crate is off-limits. Your child must not enter it, and he must leave the dog alone when she's inside. If your dog isn't crate-trained, see chapter 10 for some advice on acclimating her to one. Do so before the baby arrives. You'll be glad you did.

An exercise you can do in anticipation of having a creeper or toddler who might bug your dog while she's eating is to practice a simple food-safety exercise. Brian Kilcommons and Sarah Wilson outline this in *Childproofing Your Dog*. The idea is that you teach the dog to enjoy someone approaching her bowl.

Start by feeding your dog one short helping of her food at a time. When she finishes the small amount you give her, add another small portion, repeating this until her ration of food is gone.

Next, start adding food while she is actually eating, until she is completely relaxed with your being around her food bowl. Then, put down her whole meal at once, but go to her bowl a few times during the meal to add a delicious tidbit, like a piece of cheese or meat. Speak to her kindly as you do this.

For the next few days, stroke her gently while you add the tidbits. The next step (and we're almost finished) is to pick up her bowl while she's eating, take it away, and add the delicious tidbit. Immediately put it back down, and stay to stroke her for a while. Once she is relaxed while you're doing this, put your hand in her bowl while she's eating. You're imitating what just might happen (despite your best efforts) with a little one around. You're also creating a dog that can handle such an intrusion.

Dog-Proofing Your Child

As your baby grows, he needs to be taught some ground rules about how to behave around dogs. "One of the rules I set is that if the dog moves away from the child, the child is not allowed to pursue it," says author Wilson. The dog knows that she has to do no more than get up and move if she wants to be left alone. If you allow your child to pursue the dog, she points out, then the dog has no recourse except to growl or snarl. If that happens, says Wilson, "it falls 100 percent on your shoulders."

Another important rule Wilson recommends is not to allow your child to do to a dog what you wouldn't allow him to do to another child. Your dog will likely be upset if your child provokes her, so your child must be taught to respect the dog just as he should respect another member of the family.

Adding a Dog to Your Family

If you have kids but want to make the family complete by adding a dog, be sure you're ready. Reread chapter 1, and search your soul. No matter how much they beg for one, don't get a dog for the kids, Wilson says. Get the dog for the family. "Mom has to want the dog, because Mom's going to be the one to care for the dog," says Wilson. If you're the mother, don't let yourself be talked into a dog if you don't want one. "A canine can bring a great deal of joy into your life," Wilson says, "and a great deal of complication, depending on your perspective."

Mother and dog owner Barbara O'Rourke agrees. Her twins, Erin and Kathleen, now nine, are dog-crazy and help with the dogs' care. But O'Rourke doesn't expect that they won't have to be reminded to take care of the dogs. If you let your kids talk you into getting a dog and try to hold them to their promises to take care of him, you're asking for trouble. If the kids don't come through (which they probably won't), they're being set up for failure, the dogs suffer, and family tensions mount. "Go ahead and get yourself a dog," says O'Rourke, "but don't expect that calling it the kids' dog will make it their responsibility."

How old should your children be before you add a dog to the family? Your child should have motor skills, Wilson says, lest a friendly pat turns into a whack on the dog's head. You should also wait until your child exhibits some ability for self-control. "That can be four or six; it depends on the child," Wilson says. A child can't follow the rules of behavior around dogs unless he has self-control.

While the dog shouldn't be made the kids' sole responsibility, they can certainly help with the dog's care, Wilson points out. Even little ones can be asked to monitor the dog's water dish and let you know when it needs filling. When they are a little older, they can do the filling themselves. Kids can also help with training by giving the dogs commands and having you do the follow-through. The children can help with grooming by participating in a weekly check of the dog to detect mats in the coat, ears that need cleaning, or toenails that need trimming.

Wilson warns against giving the kids all the lousy chores. "That's a great way to get them to resent stuff," she says. Share the less pleasant tasks, like scooping the yard. "If you want to teach your kids responsibility, then get out there and scoop the yard, too."

One job you shouldn't let your kids perform is walking the dog. There are too many unknowns out there, and if a dog saw something that made him lunge and pulled the leash from your child's hand, disaster could ensue.

My sister-in-law, Linda Brotsky, went to the animal shelter with her family when she was six years old to select a new dog. "I will never forget," says Brotsky, who now lives in Akron, Ohio, "we picked out this little black-and-white dog, and I begged my dad to let me hold the leash and walk him." The family was still in front of the animal shelter when the dog pulled the leash out of the little girl's hand and ran into the street and was killed by a car. It's not easy for a child to get over a trauma like that. "No child should ever have to experience that nightmare," Brotsky says. "I blamed myself for a long time."

If your child wants to walk the dog, then put two leashes on the dog, Wilson advises. Each of you can hold one. Your child gets the satisfaction of holding the leash, while you make sure that everyone stays safe. If you have a fenced yard, you can leash the dog and let your child hold it, provided you keep an eye on them to make sure neither is pulling the other too much.

Safety is the most important consideration when it comes to having kids and dogs in the same household. Because canines can inflict harm, and because kids don't necessarily have the sensibilities to prevent them from provoking the dog, it's up to you to be sure that all are kept safe. If not, it will be hard to live with the consequences.

24 It's a Lifetime Commitment

It's a big deal to bring a dog into your life. That's why chapter 1 urges you to carefully consider whether you're ready for a dog and exactly what type best suits you. No matter what age the dog is you bring into your life, she's almost guaranteed to bond with you—and love you unconditionally. It's one of the many endearing qualities about dogs that makes us enjoy them so much.

If you sever the tie between you and your dog, you're letting her down, and you're adding to the homeless pet problem. (Even if you find a new home for your dog, it's a home that could potentially go to another animal.) When you acquire a dog, make a lifetime commitment to her, and try to keep it!

▸ DON'T GIVE UP ON YOUR DOG ◂

The sad truth is that, for many people, dogs are disposable commodities. But they're so much more than commodities. They're living, breathing, feeling creatures that become attached to the people they live with.

Dogs are remarkably resilient, and many do well in more than one home. Our dog, Scout, was three when she joined our family and she bonded with us instantly. But many, many dogs who find themselves homeless either end up dying on the streets or are humanely euthanized in shelters. If more people tried to solve problems with their dogs rather than just give them up, fewer animals would suffer.

This is one reason I admire people who work in dog rescue. These folks—usually volunteers—foster, and help to place dogs who are homeless. Some people work specifically with one breed or type of dog. Others work with any breed, or a mix of breeds. Rescue people—as well as the folks who work in animal shelters—have one-on-one contact with people who give up their animals. It must be difficult not to express disappointment in the decisions people make.

Moving with Dogs

According to the National Council on Pet Population Study and Policy, the number one reason people turn their dogs (or their cats, for that matter) over to shelters is relocation. It can be difficult to find a rental house or apartment that will take pets (thanks to irresponsible pet owners who let their pets destroy rental property). But that's no reason to give up your dog.

If you find yourself faced with a move, try to show your dog off in the best possible light. Impress the potential landlord with your dog's titles. Every canine, purebred or otherwise, is eligible to take the Canine Good Citizen test, which is offered by the American Kennel Club. Passing that test, which demonstrates that the dog has basic manners and can comport himself properly in public, might help to convince a landlord to take a chance on you and your dog. The AKC sends you a certificate you can photocopy and attach to your rental application. If you've put any titles on your dog, be sure to brag about them. It will also reflect well if you and your dog do any therapy work, for example, visiting nursing homes, hospitals, or similar facilities.

The San Francisco SPCA has an Open Door program that lists pet-friendly rentals in San Francisco, as well as advises pet owners on finding housing. The group recommends that you create for your dog a resumé that summarizes her best qualities and shows off your responsible care for her. The SFSPCA also recommends attaching letters of reference for your dog from current and previous landlords and/or neighbors; certificates of completion of any training classes; and references from your pet's trainer, groomer, or vet. You can even attach a picture, if you think it will work to your best advantage. The SFSPCA has sample pet resumés on its Web site, www.sfspca.org.

It can be a challenge for pet owners to find rental housing, but it's not impossible. Don't let this be a reason for giving up your dog.

Training and Behavioral Problems

If you're thinking of giving up your pet because of training or behavioral problems, seek professional assistance. A good trainer or behaviorist may be able to help. It could be as simple as providing your dog with more exercise (see chapter 8) or sending him to doggie day care (see chapter 6). If your dog is acting aggressively, think twice before finding him a new home. It's not fair to pass along a dangerous dog to someone else. Get an assessment of your dog's temperament from a qualified behaviorist. If your dog is deemed so aggressive that there's nothing you can do for him, the best thing is probably to euthanize him. If the assessment indicates that there are measures you can take to alleviate the problem, it may not be necessary to give him up.

When the Dog Takes a Back Seat to Your Kids

Nothing breaks my heart more than the senior dog, once the treasured "four-legged child" of a couple, who is now ignored after a baby is born. The withdrawal of attention frequently leads to the animal's bad behavior, which leads to fear for the child's safety, which leads to getting rid of the dog. If you're a dog owner who is expecting a first child, prepare yourselves and your dog for your new arrival. Make arrangements for your dog's care, and don't ignore her. Your child has a wonderful opportunity to grow up with a loving dog. It may take some effort on your part—during a time when you have fewer hours than ever and are sleep-deprived to boot—but please remember the love and devotion your dog has given you before you decide to give up on him. (See chapter 23 for more information on integrating children into a family that already includes dogs.)

Your Dog Becomes Disabled or Terminally Ill

If your dog is injured or ill, and, as a result, loses a sense (like vision or hearing) or a limb, don't despair. Many disabled dogs lead happy lives. If you're confronted with this situation and need advice, contact Dogs With Disabilities (see the

Resources section), an organization that provides support for people with disabled dogs. If your dog is deaf, check out the book *Living with a Deaf Dog* by Susan Cope Becker, and the Deaf Dog Education Action Fund Web site at www.deafdogs.org. There's also plenty of information available for owners of blind dogs. A good place to start is www.blinddogs.com.

If your dog becomes paralyzed or terminally ill, and his needs are beyond those you can handle—assuming that his quality of life is still high—there may be an alternative to euthanasia. Angel's Gate Hospice and Rehabilitation Center for Companion Animals in Fort Salonga, New York, takes in paralyzed and dying animals. Owner Susan Marino provides holistic rehabilitative care for paralyzed animals, and keeps the terminally ill animals comfortable and happy for their remaining time. If you are faced with this scenario, contact Angel's Gate to see if the group can help.

Sometimes It Can't Be Avoided

Sue Sternberg, who also owns Rondout Valley Animals for Adoption, a small animal shelter in Accord, New York, has learned not to judge the person who gives up her dog. "Things happen," she says. "Sometimes it is a generous decision to give animals up." Most people have legitimate reasons for not keeping their animal, she says, and most people are devastated by that decision.

If finding another home for your dog is the most generous thing you can do for her, then take the time to find the new home yourself. Don't dump your animal. A neighbor left his rottweiler mix, George, tied up to a fence in Prospect Park, confident that a warm-hearted dog lover would take him in. He did not leave the dog water or any other comfort.

It turns out he was right: Warm-hearted dog lovers did take his dog in and, after a great deal of effort and a couple of false tries, they found a new home for George. My neighbor's actions were cruel and callous—cruel to the abandoned dog and cruel to the people who discovered him and could not leave him in the park. Their lives were turned upside down by this unanticipated rescue. On top of it all, my neighbor has to live with the uncertainty of not knowing what happened to the dog he once loved.

If you must give up your dog, don't take him to the shelter. Animal shelters that euthanize when they run out of space are kept busy enough by stray animals.

By taking your animal there, you might be hastening the death of another. If you take your dog to a no-kill shelter, then a golden spot is taken from a stray. No-kill shelters, which do not euthanize because they lack space, are frequently full, and can take no more animals.

Instead, find a responsible, loving home for your dog. If your dog is purebred, your first call should be to his breeder. If the breeder doesn't come through, find a good home yourself. When Janine Latus Musick, of Columbia, Missouri, came to the difficult decision to find a new home for her two yellow Labs, Cody and Claire, she herself set out to find them their new home. She was determined that the two- and three-year-old dogs would be kept together. Musick consulted the Web site of a local nonprofit animal-welfare organization, Miller-Roth (www.geocities.com/~miller-roth), and followed its guidelines for finding a new home for her pets.

Miller-Roth recommends prescreening potential adopters on the phone by asking detailed questions about their pet-owning history, as well as taking down their vet and landlord's names as references. Be critical, and check references before allowing the potential adopters to see the dog. Follow your instincts, and don't adopt your dog to anyone you don't feel comfortable with. When you make a selection, insist upon delivering the dog so that you can see firsthand where she will be living.

If you can't find a good home for your dog, you may have to consider having her euthanized. "A bad home is *not* better than no home at all," declares the Miller-Roth guidelines.

While Musick initially had some difficulty finding one home where both dogs could dwell, she followed the Miller-Roth guidelines and found a loving family in the country. "They now live on 50 acres with a duck-filled pond. Their primary jobs are to love their elderly but energetic owners and to chase off varmints," Musick says. She has even visited the dogs to see how well they're doing.

If you must give up your dog, do the right thing: Find a carefully screened, loving home for her. It's the least you can do.

Extending Your Commitment

Your commitment to your dog might extend beyond your own lifetime. We're accustomed to thinking that we'll outlive our pets, but we should make arrangements for our animals, in advance, should they outlive us. It's an important thing to do, even if it's difficult to think about our own mortality.

Select someone to care for your dog in the event you die or become incapacitated. It's a big commitment for someone to make to your pet, and you're placing much trust in this person. When a friend asked us to care for her miniature poodle should she pass away, Barry and I gave the request the same careful consideration we did when a relative asked us to be the guardians of her son should she and her husband die.

It's probably a good idea to establish a backup person in the event that life circumstances change for your first choice.

Once you've decided who will care for your dog, it should be written into your will. Under the law, animals are personal property, which means you can't leave your estate to your pet. But you can leave money for your animal's care.

Laws vary by state. In most, you cannot leave money in trust for the care of an animal. You may end up leaving money to an individual whom you've selected

▼ POOCH POINTER ▼

PLACES YOU CAN TURN TO WHEN YOU HAVE A CRISIS WITH YOUR PET

(See the Resources section for contact information)

- *your dog's breeder (a good breeder will take back one of her puppies at any time)*
- *a dog behaviorist (if you have a behavioral problem)*
- *the San Francisco SPCA (for tips on finding housing when you have a dog)*
- *breed rescue (if your dog is an American Kennel Club breed, check with the AKC for the national rescue coordinator)*
- *Dogs with Disabilities (to seek advice if your dog is disabled)*
- *Angel's Gate Hospice and Rehabilitation Center for Companion Animals (if your pet is terminally ill or paralyzed)*
- *Animals At Risk Care Sanctuary (a retirement home for animals when their owners have died)*

to care for your dog. You and that friend should understand that the money you've left is to care for your canine friend. (Obviously, this is someone you trust!) You can certainly leave your animal to someone, without attaching money to your bequest. Then it becomes a gift of personal property.

Another option is to leave money to an organization to take care of your pet. Check with your local SPCA or humane society. The SPCA of Texas, for example, has established Life Care Cottages, where animals are cared for if a minimum amount of money is bequeathed to the group. For a smaller gift, the organization will place your dog with a loving foster family, and monitor her care for life. A group in your community may have a similar program.

You could bequeath your pet to a facility specifically designed to care for animals after their owners have died. The Animals At Risk Care Sanctuary, in Modesto, California, is an example of an organization that provides a lifetime refuge for pets. Animals left to the sanctuary, a nonprofit group staffed by volunteers, live out their lives in a permanent, homelike setting. The group refers to itself as a "retirement home." Your animal's stay there is funded by fees associated with the bequest. See the Resources section for contact information.

You might also plan for the care of your pets in the event that you become seriously ill or disabled and are unable to care for them. Alpha Affiliates, Inc., a nonprofit organization dedicated to promoting the bonds between people and animals, provides an "advance directive for pet care" for the purpose of stipulating who will care for your pets in the event that you are incapacitated.

When you take in a dog, make your commitment to him a commitment for the rest of his life—even if he outlives you.

25 When It's Time to Say Good-Bye

Hands down, the single worst thing about dogs is that they don't live long enough. The healthiest canine hardly lives twenty years, and many don't make it half that long. As hard as it is to contemplate our dog's death, we'll do them—and ourselves—a favor by preparing ourselves while our dogs are still healthy.

▸ DON'T HANG ON TOO LONG ◂

Deciding to euthanize (or "put to sleep") a beloved animal friend is agonizing. You worry, are you doing the right thing? Is it really time for him to die?

"I've always found that if you have a critically ill or injured animal, and you wait long enough [to euthanize] so that there is absolutely no doubt in your mind, then you've probably waited too long," says Myrna Milani, who also wrote *Preparing for the Loss of Your Pet.*

That said, Milani asserts, you must make a decision that is right for you. If you allow someone else to pressure you or guilt you into putting your animal down, you will have a more difficult time coping with the loss. You and your family members are doubtless closer to your dog than anyone else. Who better than you would be able to sense if your animal is ready? Trust yourself and your instincts. Listen to what your dog is telling you.

Phyllis DeGioia of Madison, Wisconsin, had to euthanize her beloved fifteen-year-old mixed-breed, Berkeley, during the time I was writing this book. Berkeley had suffered two strokes in five days. "After the second one, I found her in the morning, cowering, confused, and sick; I held up her head and looked at her face closely," DeGioia recalls. "She clearly gave me a look that said she didn't want to do this anymore. It was the clearest communication I've ever seen from her." That certainty gave DeGioia the strength to euthanize her beloved dog—and it also helped her with the grieving process.

Preparing Yourself

The single best thing you can do to help yourself when you're faced with a decision about how to care for your ill or injured animal is to prepare yourself *now*. With a clear head, not one clouded by panic or guilt, think about the criteria that would have a bearing on your animal's quality of life. It's a highly individual decision, specific to you and your beliefs, as well as to the type of life your dog enjoys. For example, if your dog's whole life has been about retrieving, you might consider mobility to be an important quality-of-life issue.

People tend to be prepared for two outcomes if their dog is injured or falls ill: Either the dog will die, they imagine, or he'll recover. But sometimes the outcome falls into the gray area: There's potential for recovery but with a great deal of expensive treatment, or partial recovery with a lifestyle change for dog and owner. Then it becomes more difficult. Thinking about this in advance can help.

It's when you don't plan and end up making your decision during a time of panic, that you make choices you regret later. Milani says that when she was practicing traditional veterinary medicine (she now has a bond/behavior consulting practice), she was devastated by the number of pet owners whose years of happy memories were overshadowed by two terrible weeks at the end of the pet's life as they tried fruitlessly to save the animal.

DeGioia had given a good deal of thought about the criteria she would use in deciding whether to euthanize Berkeley. Planning ahead and letting go at the right time helped her to ease any potential guilt. "I can't imagine how much worse it would be if I were second-guessing my decision, wondering if I'd done it too early, or possibly done it too late. I would be angry with myself if I let her suffer, because I selfishly wanted her around me longer than she wanted to be," DeGioia says.

Talk to Your Vet in Advance

Milani encourages veterinarians to discuss euthanasia during routine geriatric exams. This allows you to learn your vet's beliefs about euthanasia and how he copes with it; to find out what the options are for dealing with the corpse; and to make your wishes known to your vet. Do you want heroic efforts to be made in order to save your animal?

If something should happen to your dog while you are at work, or while your dog was under someone else's care, you would want your vet to know your wishes. You can even prepare an advanced directive—like the living will you might have for yourself—so that your wishes are presented in writing.

When you're talking with your veterinarian about the eventuality that your dog will die, discuss whether you would be allowed to stay in the room with her during the euthanasia procedure. Most veterinarians will allow this request.

Many people want to be with their dog when his last breath is taken. DeGioia, for one, was glad she was there. "I stayed composed, talked to her calmly, and didn't cry. It was the *only* time in her life that she was well behaved at the vet's office. She knew it would make all the pain and suffering go away."

Other people find it too difficult to be present during the procedure. You should do what feels right for you. "If you don't want to be there, you are not going to help the animal by being there," says Milani. "The animal will pick up on your anxiety." Some people prefer not to be present during the euthanasia but want to spend some time with the body afterward. Many vets will accommodate this wish as well. Again, it's an individual decision, and you shouldn't let anyone pressure you into doing something you're uncomfortable with. Thinking about this ahead of time and deciding what you want to do is better than making a snap decision you'll have to live with forever.

Not all vets are comfortable euthanizing pets. Some, like no-kill shelters, don't believe in it, says Milani. That's something you want to know before your pet becomes gravely ill. Vets are only human—and some are freaked out by death. If you know in advance that you have a vet who, for example, freezes up when faced with euthanasia, you might want to request another vet, or bring along someone who will provide the support you need. "Without a doubt, euthanasia is the most difficult thing veterinarians do," Milani says. "It is unfortunate that it's the thing they get the least amount of training for."

When it comes time for you to euthanize your pet, feel free to request the veterinarian you would like to do the procedure. Make an appointment in advance. Don't just drop in to the vet's office. Some veterinarians will make house calls to put your dog to sleep.

What to Do with the Body

Again, it's a good idea to give some thought in advance to what you want to do with your dog's body after he dies. Your vet can dispose of it for you, or if local laws allow, you can take the body home to bury it. You can also choose to bury your pet in a pet cemetery. Do your homework about such cemeteries to make sure you're contracting with a reputable one.

The Association for Pet Loss and Bereavement (APLB) provides a listing of cemeteries that belong to the International Association of Pet Cemeteries and/or the Accredited Pet Cemetery Society. Access that listing, as well as a variety of information about coping with pet loss, at the APLB's Web site: www.aplb.org.

Another option is to have your animal cremated and the ashes returned to you. Cremation is a surprisingly expensive procedure, says Milani, since high temperatures are required to break the body down into ashes. Often pets are cremated in groups. In that case, you might get ashes back from the group cremation that represent your animal but aren't actually his ashes. Or you may get no ashes at all. If you want your dog's actual ashes to be returned to you, arrange with your vet, in advance, for an individual cremation.

If you cremate your pet, and have her ashes returned, then you have to make a decision about what to do with the ashes. Some people sprinkle them in a significant area. Others put them in a special urn or box and keep them in the house. When Mary Osterberg of Portland, Oregon, lost her beloved dog,

Maynard, to cancer, she had her cremated and kept her ashes in an urn. Exactly seven months later, Maynard's best friend, a cat named Tabitha, died. Osterberg combined the two animals' ashes in the urn and placed two nameplates on it. "Maynard was my heart and Tabitha was my soul," she says. "They belong together."

Some people keep special mementos of their dog's life, like a collar or favorite toy, near the ashes or in a keepsake box. Others bury their dog and place a special grave marker at the site. Again, this is a highly personal decision, one that bears thinking about in advance.

Coping with Your Grief

If you plan ahead for your pet's death, you'll probably have an easier time coping with the loss. If, while your dog is still healthy, you face the reality that he will die, you're less likely to have made any decision that you might feel guilty about. "Guilt is the most devastating emotion in the human/pet relationship," says Milani.

One of the difficulties in coping with the devastating loss of a cherished animal companion is that people who are not pet lovers cannot understand the depth of your grief. Callous comments like "he was just a dog" or "why don't you just go out and get another one?" can be hurtful.

The Association for Pet Loss and Bereavement (APLB) offers a list of qualified counselors who specialize in pet loss to help you work through your grief. It also provides a list of hot lines that are affiliated with established organizations, like veterinary schools, as well as a list of support groups. You might feel isolated in your grief, and fear that no one can understand. But there is a world of hope out there, and the APLB Web site offers a great starting place for finding it. If you don't have Internet access, call the APLB at (718) 832-0690. Another resource to help you in your grief is the Iams Pet Loss Support Resource Center. You can call it toll-free at 1-888-332-7738; you'll be given the number of the pet-loss support line nearest you.

Everyone grieves differently. As she copes with her own loss, DeGioia advises others to let out their emotions. "All your feelings about death, the ends of relationships, and saying good-bye will be affected if you don't deal with it. Fall apart, cry, scream, whine, yell, but get it out," she suggests. "Nature designed most of our pets to have such different life spans. I think one of the reasons that design was made was to help us learn how to grieve."

Getting a New Pet

Deciding whether to get a new pet after one has died is also a highly personal decision. Well-meaning friends may encourage you to get one right away, or even offer to give you one.

Don't take in a new pet until you're absolutely ready, and don't expect that pet to replace your old friend. The new pet may help fill the hole in your heart, but he's a unique animal, not a replacement. Again, don't let others influence you unduly.

You may be ready immediately, in a few months or years, or maybe never. It's your decision, one you don't have to make any excuses for.

Thinking about your dog dying isn't easy, no matter how far into the future that eventuality seems. But it's a fact that our dogs live short lives, so we should prepare for the worst. Face your fears, even if your dog is healthy. Talk to your vet and your family members. You'll be glad you did when the time for major decisions arrives.

Recommended Reading

Books

Adams, Janine. *You Can Talk to Your Animals: Animal Communicators Tell You How*. Foster City, Calif.: Howell Book House/IDG Books Worldwide, 2000.

Arden, Andrea. *Dog-Friendly Dog Training*. Foster City, Calif.: Howell Book House/IDG Books Worldwide, 2000.

Barish, Eileen. *Vacationing with Your Pet*. 4th ed. Scottsdale, Ariz.: Pet Friendly Publications, 1999.

Becker, Susan Cope. *Living with a Deaf Dog*. Cincinnati, Ohio: Susan Cope Becker, 1998.

Billinghurst, Ian. *Give Your Dog a Bone*. Lithgow, N.S.W.: Ian Billinghurst, 1993.

——. *Grow Your Pup with Bones*. Lithgow, N.S.W.: Ian Billinghurst, 1998.

Derrico, Karen. *Unforgettable Mutts: Pure of Heart, Not of Breed*. Troutdale, Ore.,: NewSage Press, 1999.

Donaldson, Jean. *The Culture Clash*. Berkeley, Calif.: James & Kenneth Publishers, 1996.

——. *Dogs Are from Neptune*. Berkeley, Calif.: James & Kenneth Publishers, 1998.

Dunbar, Ian. *Dog Behavior: An Owner's Guide to a Happy, Healthy Pet*. New York: Howell Book House, 1999.

——. *How to Teach a New Dog Old Tricks*. 2d ed. Berkeley, Calif.: James & Kenneth Publishers, 1996.

Habgood, Dawn, and Robert Habgood. *On the Road Again with Man's Best Friend (United States)*. Duxbury, Mass.: Dawbert Press, Inc., 1999. Regional editions also available.

Kilcommons, Brian, and Sarah Wilson. *Childproofing Your Dog*. New York: Warner Books, 1994.

——. *Good Owners, Great Dogs*. 2d ed. New York: Warner Books, 1999.

——. *Paws to Consider: Choosing the Right Dog for You and Your Family*. New York: Warner Books, 1999.

McKay, Pat. *Reigning Cats and Dogs.* Rev. ed. Pasadena, Calif.: Oscar Publications, 1996.

Martin, Ann. *Foods Pets Die For.* Troutdale, Ore.: NewSage Press, 1997.

Milani, Myrna. *DogSmart.* Lincolnwood, Ill.: NTC/Contemporary Publishing, 1998.

——. *The Body Language and Emotions of Dogs.* New York: William Morrow, 1993.

——. *Preparing for the Loss of Your Pet.* Rocklin, Calif.: Prima Publishing, 1998.

Miller, Cynthia D. *Canine Adventures: Fun Things To Do With Your Dog.* Yuba City, Calif.: Animalia Publishing, 1999.

Miller Pat. *The Common Sense Approach: Positive Dog Training—The Fun and Rewarding Way to Train Your Dog.* Houston: Gulf Publishing, 2000.

Palika, Liz. *The Consumer's Guide to Dog Food.* New York: Howell Book House, 1996.

Pitcairn, Richard, and Susan Hubble Pitcairn. *Dr. Pitcairn's Complete Guide to Natural Health for Dogs and Cats.* Rev. ed. Emmaus, Penn: Rodale, 1995.

Puotinen, C. J. *The Encyclopedia of Natural Pet Care.* 2d ed. Los Angeles: Keats Publishing, 2000.

Rugaas, Turid. *On Talking Terms with Dogs: Calming Signals.* Carlsborg, Wash.: Legacy By Mail, 1997.

Schultze, Kymythy. *Natural Nutrition for Dogs and Cats: The Ultimate Diet.* Carlsbad, Calif.: Hay House, 1998.

Sife, Wallace. *The Loss of a Pet.* New York: Howell Book House, 1998.

Spadafori, Gina. *Dogs for Dummies.* Foster City, Calif.: IDG Books Worldwide, 1996.

Tortora, Daniel. *The Right Dog for You.* New York: Simon & Schuster, 1983.

Walkowicz, Chris. *The Perfect Match: A Dog Buyer's Guide.* New York: Howell Book House, 1996.

Walkowicz, Chris, and Bonnie Wilcox. *Successful Dog Breeding: The Complete Handbook of Canine Midwifery.* New York: Howell Book House, 1994.

Walters, Heather MacLean. *Take Your Pet Along.* 2d ed. Chester, N.J.: M.C.E., 1997.

——. *Take Your Pet Too! Fun Things to Do!* Chester, N.J.: M.C.E., 1996.

Welton, Michele. *Your Purebred Puppy: A Buyer's Guide.* 2d edition. New York: Henry Holt, 2000.

Wood, Deborah. *Help for Your Shy Dog.* New York: Howell Book House, 1999.

——. *The Tao of Bow Wow: Understanding & Training Your Dog the Taoist Way.* New York: Dell, 1998.

Magazines and Newsletters

(Note: the contact information provided is for subscriptions.)

- *The AKC Gazette*
  American Kennel Club
  5580 Centerview Drive
  Raleigh, NC 27606-3390
  1-800-533-7323
  www.akc.org

- *The Bark*
  2810 8th Street
  Berkeley, CA 94710
  (510) 704-0827
  www.thebark.com

- *Dog Fancy*
  P. O. Box 532644
  Boulder, CO 80322-3264
  1-800-365-4421
  www.dogfancy.com

- *DogGone*
  P. O. Box 651155
  Vero Beach, FL 32965-1155
  1-888-364-8728
  www.doggonefun.com

- *Dog World*
  P. O. Box 56240
  Boulder, CO 80322-6240
  1-800-361-8056
  www.dogworldmag.com

- *Whole Dog Journal*
  P. O. Box 420235
  Palm Coast, FL 32142
  1-800-829-9125
  customer_service@belvoir.com

Resources

Acquiring a Dog

RESEARCHING A BREED, FINDING A BREEDER

- *The American Kennel Club*
  5580 Centerview Drive
  Raleigh, NC 27606
  (919) 233-9767
  Breeder referral service: (900) 407-7877
  www.akc.org

- *The American Kennel Club Library*
  260 Madison Avenue, 4th Floor
  New York, NY 10016
  (212) 696-8245

DOG CONNECTIONS: RESCUE

- www.uncc.edu/jvanoate/k9/k9rescu.html
  This site from dog lover Judith van Noate is a good place to start if you're interested in finding a rescue dog.

- *Miller-Roth*
  2000 East Broadway, #141
  Columbia, MO 65201
  (573) 657-9633
  miller-roth@geocities.com
  www.geocities.com/~miller-roth/
  This is an all-volunteer, not-for-profit, tax-exempt, no-kill organization that has been helping animals and their owners since 1989. The Web site has advice on finding a new home for your dogs.

Animal Communication

- www.animaltalk.net/newdirectory.html
  Penelope Smith's directory of interspecies telepathic communicators.

Disabled Dogs

- *Deaf Dog Education and Action Fund*
  P. O. Box 369
  Boonville, CA 95415
  www.deafdogs.org

- *Dogs with Disabilities*
  1406 East Small Lane
  Mt. Prospect, IL 60056
  (847) 296-8277
  http://members.bytemeusa.com/~dwd/

- *Owners of Blind Dogs*
  www.blinddogs.com

Dog Camps

- *Camp Gone to the Dogs*
  P. O. Box 600
  Putney, VT 05346
  (802) 387-5673
  www.campgonetothedogs.com

- *Camp Winnaribbun*
  P. O. Box 50300
  Reno, NV 89513
  (775) 348-8412
  www.campw.com

- *Dog Days of Wisconsin*
  1879 Haymarket, #24
  Waukesha, WI 53189
  1-800-226-7436
  www.dogcamp.com

- *The Dog's Camp*
  (Asheville, North Carolina)
  Catherine Mills
  7 Greenleaf Road
  Fletcher, NC 28732
  (828) 684-4814

- *Dog Scout Camp*
  Dogs Scouts of America
  5068 Nestel Road
  St. Helen, MI 48656
  (517) 389-2000
  www.dogscouts.com

Health and Food

- *Alternative and Complementary Veterinary Medicine*
  www.altvetmed.com
  Includes membership directories of the American Holistic Veterinary Medical Association, the Academy of Veterinary Homeopathy, and the International Veterinary Acupuncture Society.

- *Colorado State University's Small Animal Vaccination Protocol*
  www.cvmbs.colostate.edu/vth/savp2.html

- *Dog Foods Comparison Chart*
  home.hawaii.rr.com/wolfepack/

- *Poisonous Plants*
  cal.vet.upenn.edu/poison/index.html

- *"What's Really in Pet Food" investigative report*
  Animal Protection Institute (API)
  P. O. Box 22505
  Sacramento, CA 95822
  1-800-348-7387
  onlineapi@aol.com
  www.api4animals.org/Petfood.html

Free single copies of API reports are available via mail by calling the above number or e-mailing.

Internet mailing lists

- *Complete List of Dog-Related E-Mail Lists*
  www.k9web.com/dog-faqs/lists/email-list.html

- *Searchable Community of Lists*
  www.egroups.com

Moving with Pets

- *San Francisco SPCA's Open Door program*
  2500-16th Street
  San Francisco, CA 94103-4213
  (415) 554-3000
  www.sfspca.org
  Offers advice on finding an apartment or rental house when you have pets. Site includes sample resumés you can create for your pet.

Providing for your dog when you no longer can

- *Alpha Affiliates*
  P. O. Box 176
  Mendham, NJ 07945-0176
  AlphaAffiliates@webtv.net
  www.caninetimes.com/NonProfits/alphaafilliate
  A sample "advanced directive for pet care" to be used if you're incapacitated is available for $5.

- *Angel's Gate Hospice and Rehabilitation Center for Companion Animals*
  18 Josephine Lane
  Fort Salonga, NY 11768
  (631) 269-7641

- *Animals At Risk Care Sanctuary (AARC)*
  P. O. Box 578763
  Modesto, CA 95357
  (209) 527-2272

cjwww.csustan.edu/animals/AARC.html
A "retirement home" for animals. You can bequeath this nonprofit organization a sum of money to care for your animals in comfort after your death.

Supplies

DISCOUNT CATALOGS/SITES

- *Doctors Foster & Smith*
  2553 Air Park Road
  P. O. Box 100
  Rhinelander, WI 54501-0100
  1-800-826-7206
  www.drsfostersmith.com

- *Great Companions*
  P. O. Box 87
  Warren, MN 56762
  1-800-829-2138
  www.greatcompanions.com

- *KV Vet Supply Co.*
  P. O. Box 245
  3190 North Road
  David City, NE 68632-0245
  1-800-423-8211

- *New England Serum Company*
  P. O. Box 128
  Topsfield, MA 01938-0228
  1-800-637-3786
  www.neserum.com
  A great source for grooming equipment. Its "best buys" specials offer great bargains.

- *Pets.com*
  1-888-321-7387
  Service@pets.com
  www.pets.com

My favorite of the large e-commerce pet sites, pets.com not only offers a wide selection of discounted pet supplies, including food, but it also supplies articles by writers (like me) on a wide variety of pet-related topics. (Plus, I love the sock puppet!)

- *Valley Vet Supply Direct Pet Superstore*
  1118 Pony Express Highway
  P. O. Box 504
  Marysville, KS 66508-0504
  1-800-360-4838
  www.valleyvet.com

SPECIALTY SITES/CATALOGS

- *Dogwise*
  701 B Poplar
  P. O. Box 2778
  Wenatchee, WA 98807-2778
  1-800-776-2665
  mail@dogwise.com
  www.dogwise.com
  Formerly known as Direct Book Service, this catalog and Web site carries "cutting-edge dog books and products for serious dog enthusiasts and trainers."

- *Doggone Good*
  320-F Turtle Creek Court
  San Jose, CA 95125
  1-800-660-2665
  www.doggone.com
  info@doggonegood.com
  An on-line store with high-quality training-related merchandise and personalized customer service.

- *In the Company of Dogs*
  104 Challenger Drive
  Portland, TN 37148-1717
  1-800-924-5050

www.inthecompanyofdogs.com
High-end apparel and gear for dog lovers.

- *Legacy By Mail*
  P. O. Box 697
  Carlsborg, WA 98324
  1-888-876-9364
  info@legacy-by-mail.com
  www.legacy-by-mail.com
  Owned by dog trainer Terry Ryan, Legacy By Mail is a good source for training books, videos, and tools.

- *SitStay.com*
  4824 North 57 Street
  Lincoln, NE 68507
  1-888-467-3421
  www.sitstay.com
  A great selection of items, including natural treats, with customer service that goes the extra mile.

Training and Behavior

- *American Dog Trainers Network*
  www.inch.com/~dogs
  (212) 727-7257
  New York dog trainer Robin Kovary provides a "comprehensive, one-stop resource for dog owners, dog trainers, and the media." She also offers a free phone help line at the above number, between the hours of 1 P.M. and 3 P.M., Monday through Friday.

- *Association of Pet Dog Trainers (APDT)*
  66 Morris Avenue, Suite 2A
  Springfield, NJ 07081
  1-800-PET-DOGS
  www.apdt.com
  Contact this organization, which promotes dog-friendly training methods, to find a positive dog trainer near you. APDT also sponsors training-related conferences the public can attend.

- *Dog Play*
  www.dog-play.com
  An exhaustive and descriptive list of the many activities owners can do with their dogs.

- *Great Pets*
  www.greatpets.com
  A Web site from trainers Sarah Wilson and Brian Kilcommons, offering expert answers to readers' individual questions.

- *Puppyworks*
  P. O. Box 954
  Benecia, CA 94510
  (707) 745-4237
  events@puppyworks.com
  www.puppyworks.com
  Sponsors of dog-related conferences, seminars, and special events.

Traveling with pets

- www.petswelcome.com
- www.petvacations.com
- www.traveldog.com

Videos

- Dunbar, Ian. *Sirius Puppy Training.* 90 min. New York: Bluford & Toth Productions, 1987.

- Pryor, Karen. *Clicker Magic.* 56 min. Waltham, Mass.: Sunshine Books, 1997.

- Rugaas, Turid. *Calming Signals: What Your Dog Tells You.* 48 min. Carlsborg, Wash.: Legacy By Mail, 2000.

Index